DEPARTMENT OF THE NAVY
HEADQUARTERS UNITED STATES MARINE CORPS
3000 MARINE CORPS PENTAGON
WASHINGTON, DC 20350-3000

MARINE CORPS FLYING HOUR PROGRAM (FHP) MANAGEMENT

DEPARTMENT OF THE NAVY
HEADQUARTERS UNITED STATES MARINE CORPS
3000 MARINE CORPS PENTAGON
WASHINGTON, DC 20350-3000

MCO 3125.1B
APP
27 Apr 2009

MARINE CORPS ORDER 3125.1B

From: Commandant of the Marine Corps
To: Distribution List

Subj: MARINE CORPS FLYING HOUR PROGRAM (FHP) MANAGEMENT

Ref: (a) NAVSO P-3013
      (b) MCO 1553.1B
      (c) MCO P3500.14H
      (d) 2007 Marine Aviation Plan (AVPLAN)
      (e) OPNAVINST 3710.7T
      (f) CNRF 7100.1B
      (g) MCO P7300.19B
      (h) SECNAV M-5210.1
      (i) MCO P4400.177D
      (j) Joint Publication 1-02, Department of Defense Dictionary of
          Military and Associated Terms," April 12, 2001
      (k) OPNAVINST 5442.4M
      (l) CNO Washington DC 071535ZDEC2005 (NOTAL)
      (m) SECNAV M-5214.1
      (n) OPNAVINST 7310.1F
      (o) NAVMC DIR 3500.14

Encl: (1) Procedural Guidance for Marine Corps Flying Hour Program

Reports Required: I.   Sortie Based Training Submissions (Report Control
                         Symbol EXEMPT), encl (4), par. 2a
                   II.   Budget OPTAR Submission (Report Control Symbol
                         EXEMPT), encl (5), par. 5
                  III.   Flight Hour Cost Report (Report Control Symbol
                         EXEMPT), encl (6), par. 5a
                   IV.   Reserve Component Activation Funding (Report Control
                         Symbol EXEMPT), encl (6), par. 12c(1)

1. Situation. This Order provides policy, guidance, and responsibilities
for the execution of the Marine Corps Flight Hour Program (FHP) per
references (a) through (o).

2. Cancellation. MCO 3125.1A.

3. Mission. Plan, execute, and manage an annual Marine Corps FHP for Active
Component (AC) and Reserve Component (RC) deployable and non-deployable
squadrons that provides combat capable units and operational support to
Marine Air Ground Task Force (MAGTF) and joint force commanders.

4. Execution

   a. Commander's Intent and Concept of Operations

       (1) Commander's Intent. A primary responsibility of Marine commanders is combat readiness. Marine Corps flight operations management is composed of two elements: the Sortie Based Training Program (SBTP) and the FHP. The SBTP is the commander's execution tool and the FHP is the budgeting tool. Commanders shall utilize all available resources to ensure their commands are trained per the current editions of the appropriate Type/Model/Series (T/M/S) Training and Readiness (T&R) manuals and the FHP is managed per this Order.

       (2) Concept of Operations. The FHP provides resources for Marine aviation to train in prescribed readiness areas, perform flights in support of required maintenance and logistics efforts, and conduct routine peacetime and deployed operations. It is imperative that the Marine Aviation T&R, Core Competency Resource Model (CCRM), SBTP, Marine Corps FHP and FHP reporting are completely integrated to validate the annual Marine Corps aviation readiness and flying hour requirements.

          (a) Marine Corps FHP. The term "Flying Hour Program" refers to the allocation and obligation of funds from the Operation and Maintenance, Navy (O&M,N) and Operation and Maintenance, Navy Reserve (O&M,NR) accounts appropriated to the Marine Corps for the operation and maintenance of Marine Corps aircraft. The Deputy Commandant for Aviation (DC AVN) (APP-2) validates Marine Forces peacetime tactical aviation training requirements with the T&R, CCRM and SBTP submissions and submits them to Chief of Naval Operations (CNO) headquarters staff (OPNAV) Flying Hour Program (Code N432D). OPNAV N432D incorporates Marine requirements with the Navy's Fleet Response Plan (FRP) sortie based flying hour requirements into one OP-20 FHP budget exhibit. OPNAV N43 conducts program reviews and submits a balanced fleet (Navy/Marine Corps) aviation readiness requirement to OPNAV N80 Programming Division, for final submission to the Secretary of the Navy (SECNAV) Financial Management Branch (FMB). FMB submits the budget proposal to Congress. Once approved by Congress and signed by the President, the proposal becomes a Presidential Budget. Just prior to the fiscal year, the Navy's Total Obligated Authority is returned to FMB for distribution to the Navy's Budget Submitting Offices. The FHP has four Type Commanders (TYCOMs): Commander, Naval Air Forces Pacific (COMNAVAIRPAC); Commander, Naval Air Forces Atlantic (COMNAVAIRLANT); Commander, Naval Reserve Forces (COMNAVRESFOR); and Commander, Naval Air Forces Europe (COMNAVEUR). The FHP funds are passed to the respective TYCOM through Commander U.S. Fleet Forces (USFF); and Commander, Pacific Fleet (COMPACFLT) first, and then allocated to Marine Forces Pacific (MARFORPAC), Marine Forces Command (MARFORCOM), and Marine Forces Reserve (MARFORRES) (MARFORs) in the form of an Operating Target (OPTAR). COMNAVRESFOR passes Marine Reserve OPTAR to the Naval site comptrollers under the management of the 4th Marine Aircraft Wing (MAW) Aviation Logistics Division Comptroller (ALD-C). The programming and obligation of O&M,N and O&M,NR funds through the Naval chain of command is a formalized administrative procedure outlined in reference (a). The Marine Corps FHP is funded in four categories or schedules: tactical aircraft (TACAIR), Fleet Air Training (FAT), Fleet Air Support (FAS), and Reserves.

            1. TACAIR FHP. The TACAIR FHP encompasses all deployable AC Fixed-Wing, Rotary-Wing and Tilt-Rotor squadrons. Activated RC squadrons will be funded from the gaining MARFOR TACAIR FHP. Activated MARFORRES squadrons' O&M,NR FHP funds unexecuted because of a squadron's mobilization will be returned to Commander Naval Reserve Forces Command (CNRFC) and FMB

for reprogramming to the gaining MARFOR. Marine Aviation utilizes the CCRM integrated with the SBTP as the primary inputs for the TACAIR FHP requirement. Marine Corps tactical aviation shall maintain T-2.0 average level training readiness to be prepared to rapidly and effectively deploy on short notice for OPLAN or contingency operations. Funding for the TACAIR FHP is displayed in the OP-20 Schedule A in chapter 1.

    2. FAT FHP. The FAT FHP encompasses the Marine Corps Fleet Replacement Squadrons (FRS). This schedule is based upon annual FRS aircrew throughput requirements, published as the Marine Corps Pilot Training Rate in the annual aircrew Training & Education Command (TECOM) Fiscal Year Training Implementation Plan (TIP), which is provided to OPNAV N782B as outlined in reference (b). OPNAV N782B publishes a requirements letter, which is provided to OPNAV N43 for programming in the OP-20. Funding for the FAT FHP is displayed in the OP-20 schedule B at chapter 1.

    3. FAS FHP. The FAS FHP encompasses deployable and non-deployable AC Operational Support Airlift (OSA), Search and Rescue, and Marine Helicopter Squadron 1 (HMX-1) aircraft. FAS hours are calculated using historical operational, support, and aircrew training requirements. Funding for the FAS FHP is displayed in the OP-20 Schedule C in chapter 1.

    4. Reserves FHP. The Reserves FHP encompasses all deployable and non-deployable RC Fixed-Wing, Rotary-Wing and Tilt-Rotor squadrons and OSA aircraft. Reserve hours are calculated using the minimum aircrew readiness requirements and operational commitments. Funding for the Reserve FHP is displayed in the OP-20 schedule D in Chapter 1 under the total Chief Naval Reserves (CNR) requirement.

    (b) T&R Program. The Marine Aviation T&R Program, reference (c), guides the development of unit warfighting capabilities by providing commanders with standardized programs of instruction for training all aviation aircrew through community T&R syllabi. These syllabi are based on specific performance standards designed to ensure units maintain proficiency in core skills and combat leadership. Aviation T&R models are used to standardize T&R Program methodology and to provide a direct link between aviation training, readiness, requirements, and resources. The two models used are the Core Competency Model and the CCRM.

    1. Core Competency Model. Also known as the Core Model, the Core Competency Model establishes the basic structure around which each T&R Program is created. It links community Mission Statements, Mission Essential Tasks Lists, core capability statements, core capability and combat leadership requirements. All community T&R Manuals follow the core competency model structure but the requirements and metrics are tailored to the specific needs of the community.

    2. CCRM. The Marine Corps CCRM directly links the T&R Program with the USMC FHP and Status of Resources and Training System readiness reporting programs. The CCRM generates annual sortie and flying hour requirements (broken down by training, support, and operational hour category) for maintaining selected T-Level readiness ratings for each tactical aviation squadron. Each community's CCRM reflects the core model as defined in its respective T&R manual. See chapter 2 for detailed CCRM information.

    (c) SBTP. The Marine Corps SBTP concept was first introduced in the Marine Aviation Campaign Plan (MACP) and is continued in the Marine Aviation Plan (AVPLAN), reference (d). The intent of the SBTP is to allow squadron commanders to develop an executable sortie based training plan that reflects their unit's training exercise and employment plan and T&R requirements to provide combat ready units for the MAGTF. The SBTP focus is on training to the core competencies of each T/M/S aircraft and emphasizes the units' core competencies over individual training goals while wisely managing aircraft utilization. The standardized format for forecasting and reporting unit FHPs surpasses previous SBTP models. The standardized Marine Corps-wide definition of a sortie, in accordance with reference (e), is detailed in chapter 3, to include the aforementioned SBTP reporting formats and procedures.

   b. Subordinate Element Missions. FHP management requires the assignment of the following responsibilities.

      (1) Deputy Commandant for Aviation (DC AVN). DC AVN is the HQMC Aviation Combat Element FHP advocate and is responsible for overall management of the Marine Corps FHP, to include the following.

         (a) Advocate Marine Corps FHP requirements within the Department of the Navy's (DON) planning, programming, budgeting, and execution process and maintain oversight of Marine Forces FHP execution and reporting.

         (b) Review MARFORCOM, MARFORPAC, and MARFORRES TACAIR, FAT, FAS, and Reserve submissions ensuring they meet Marine Corps requirements. Submit the AC and RC FHP to OPNAV N-43 per chapter 2.

         (c) Provide MARFORs with a monthly FHP execution update, displaying hours, from both Naval Aviation Logistics Command/Management Information System (NALCOMIS) and OP-20 databases, broken down into training, support, operational, and contingency categories, as well as the cost per flight hour and hour per crew per month (H/C/M).

         (d) Inform the Deputy Commandant for Programs and Resources of shortfalls in funding which could adversely affect the Marine Corps FHP.

         (e) Evaluate waivers for pilots unable to meet annual flying hour minimums.

         (f) Act on all requests for waiver of Duty Involving Flight Denied (DIFDEN) status in cases where it is advantageous for MAGTF staff aviators to fly in support of operational flying units.

         (g) Oversee the reprogramming of unexecuted activated 4th MAW unit FHP funds to the gaining AC MARFORs and act as Marine Corps advocate to FMB and the Office of the Secretary of Defense (OSD) during this process.

      (2) Deputy Commandant for Manpower & Reserve Affairs (DC M&RA)

         (a) Staff tactical aircraft squadrons at a manning level of 90 percent of Table of Organization in accordance with the MACP and funding assumptions within the OP-20. This policy will accomplish the following.

            (1) Ensure funded TACAIR billets are filled to the maximum extent possible.

            (2) Provide consistency between reported manpower data, quarterly Operational Tempo reports, and authorized manning. The DON FMB tracks unit manning, and corresponding fiscal restrictions are made in the FHP to compensate for manning at less than authorized levels. Manning

squadrons at authorized levels will ensure that no unnecessary decrements are taken within the FHP budget.

(b) Ensure all aviators assigned to MAGTF Headquarters and joint staffs are assigned in a DIFDEN status.

(3) <u>Deputy Commandant for Programs and Resources (DC P&R)</u>. Serve as alternate point of contact for Marine Corps FHP on technical budget/fiscal matters. Assist DC AVN in adjudicating unresolved aviation budgetary issues.

(4) <u>Commanding General (CG), TECOM</u>

(a) Provide Marine Corps FRS requirements, in Replacement Aircrew equivalents for flight students per the Future Year Defense Plan TIP and total flying hour/sortie requirements, by T/M/S aircraft, to OPNAV N789 for use in the development of the FAT FHP.

(b) Maintain the CCRM ensuring its consistency with the current community T&Rs per chapter 2.

(5) <u>COMMARFORPAC, COMMARFORCOM</u>. Function as the FHP resource sponsor, oversight authority, and TYCOM level representative.

(a) Review proposed MAW SBTP and authorize flight hour funding to support the approved MARFOR FHP.

(b) Effect liaison with Commander, Naval Air Forces and maintain responsibility for presenting, monitoring, and defending all budgetary actions to TYCOM/OPNAV/Headquarters Marine Corps (HQMC).

(c) Submit required Marine Corps Sierra-Hotel Aviation Readiness Program (M-SHARP) SBTP reports to HQMC (APP-2) per chapter 3.

(d) Facilitate assignment of OPTAR grants to subordinate units and monitor and supervise execution of those grants.

(e) Assist subordinate units in developing program requirements and determine actions to be taken when funds are inadequate to execute approved FHP.

(f) Approve all contracts involving manpower and contract maintenance in accordance with chapter 6.

(g) Upon assuming operational control (OPCON) of activated RC squadrons, request supplemental OP-20 O&M,N funds to support funding the FHP of those squadrons.

(h) Allocate funding for and report all activated RC squadron flight hours per enclosures (6) and (7).

(6) <u>COMMARFORRES</u>. Function as the Reserve FHP resource sponsor, oversight authority, and TYCOM level representative to CNR.

(a) Review Reserve FHP requirements and submit to HQMC (APP-2) prior to submission to CNRFC.

(b) Submit required M-SHARP SBTP reports to HQMC (APP-2) per chapter 3.

(c) Ensure activated RC squadrons assigned OPCON to MARFORCOM or MARFORPAC track and account for flight hours per chapter 5.

(d) Facilitate assignment of OPTAR grants to subordinate units and monitor execution of those grants.

(e) Assist subordinate units in developing program requirements and determine actions to be taken when funds are inadequate to execute approved program.

(f) Report all activated units' unexecuted flight hour funds to CNRFC and FMB for reprogramming per chapter 5.

(g) Approve all contracts involving manpower and contract maintenance per chapter 6.

(7) CG, 1st/2d/3d MAW

(a) Provide oversight on subordinate units' SBTPs and TACAIR FHPs to ensure they provide the sorties per aircrew required to attain the Core Skill Proficient (CSP) and combat leadership aircrew necessary to achieve a T-2.0 average level of readiness.

(b) Ensure participation in the TACAIR FHP is limited to the TACAIR squadron and augment pilots necessary to meet readiness goals and operational commitments. Ensure all TACAIR staff aircrew maintain readiness minimums prescribed in reference (e).

(c) Assign all first tour aviators to TACAIR squadrons for at least 2 years prior to reassignment within the MAW.

(d) Provide HQMC (APP-2) annual unit SBTP projections and monthly execution data per chapter 3.

(e) Perform accounting and reporting for OPTAR assigned by the TYCOM/MARFOR using the procedures per chapter 4.

(f) Endorse requests for waivers of the minimum flying requirements for those aviators not able to make annual flying minimums.

(g) Monitor the FAT FHP requirement and execution for assigned FRSs.

(h) Provide a quarterly status of funds report by fund code, authorization, obligation, and balance to the MARFORs.

(8) CG, 4th MAW

(a) Manage reporting for OPTAR assigned by CNRFC N-8 using the procedures per reference (f) and chapter 5.

(b) Ensure all site comptrollers/squadrons report data to CNRFC N-8 per reference (f).

(c) Ensure Monthly Flight Hour Cost Report (FHCR) numbers match between all site comptrollers, G-3 and NALCOMIS. Submit required reports to HQMC (APP-2) per chapter 5.

(d) Ensure all contracts involving manpower/contract maintenance receives CNRFC N-8 approval per reference (f).

(e) Report unexecuted flight hours for all activated units to CNRFC N-8 for reprogramming and ensure all activated units attached to a MARFOR track and account for flight hours per chapter 4.

(f) Assist subordinate units in developing program requirements and determine actions to be taken when funds are inadequate to execute approved program.

(g) Review Reserve FHP requirements to maintain unit readiness to meet required training and support requirements.

(h) Provide HQMC (APP-2) annual unit SBTP projections and monthly execution data per chapter 3.

(i) Ensure activated squadrons attached to MARFORCOM or MARFORPAC track and account for flight hours per chapter 4.

(9) Commander, Marine Corps Installations East (MCI-East); Commander, Marine Corps Installations West (MCI-West), and Commander, Marine Corps Bases Japan

(a) Provide annual FAS flying hour requirements to the Commander, MARFORCOM/MARFORPAC.

(b) Receive funding from MARFOR and distribute to air station commands as required.

(c) Provide financial management reports to the MARFOR.

(d) Provide HQMC (APP-2) annual unit SBTP projections and monthly execution data per chapter 3.

(e) Provide a weekly status of funds report by fund code, authorization, obligation, and balance to the MARFOR.

(10) Commanding Officer (CO), Marine Aircraft Group (MAG)

(a) Monitor unit STBPs and TACAIR FHP planning and execution. Monitor FAT, FHP planning and execution, if applicable.

(b) Ensure all FHP funds are expended in accordance with reference (g) and chapter 4.

(c) Ensure squadron Budget OPTAR Report (BOR) inputs and NALCOMIS flight hour totals match on a monthly basis. Report initial disparities between the BOR and NALCOMIS flight hours to MAW G-3/Comptroller/Aviation Logistics Department.

(d) Provide accurate SBTP projection and execution data per chapter 3.

(11) CO, Marine Aviation Logistics Squadron (MALS)

(a) Ensure all Operational Functional Category (OFC) funds received from the MAG fiscal officer are administered properly by the MALS

Aviation Supply Officer (AvnSupO) in accordance with applicable directives and chapter 4.

(b) Ensure the AvnSupO has established positive controls to avoid the over-obligation or over-expenditure of funds.

(c) Ensure all contracts involving manpower/contract maintenance receives MARFOR approval per chapter 6.

(d) Ensure squadron BOR and NALCOMIS flight hour totals match on a monthly basis and ensure any discrepancies are corrected prior to totals going forward to the MAW G-3 and TYCOM.

(12) CO, Squadron

(a) Plan and execute unit SBTP to maintain the requisite number of CSP and combat leadership aircrews for T-2.0 readiness levels per unit T&R Core Competency Model.

(b) Ensure aircrew log flight hours per chapter 4.

(c) Ensure the Operations Chief and Maintenance Analyst reconcile unit flight hour totals daily, ensuring that the BOR and NALCOMIS data match exactly. Any discrepancies are to be corrected prior to the totals going forward to the MALS Analyst and MAG fiscal department.

(d) Provide accurate SBTP projection and execution data per chapter 3.

(13) CO, Reserve Site

(a) Ensure all FHP funds are entered and obligated in Fund Administration and Standardized Data Automation (FASTDATA) before releasing into supply system in accordance with chapter 5.

(b) Ensure squadron Flight Hour Cost Report (FHCR) and NALCOMIS flight hour totals match on a monthly basis and provide an accurate submission of monthly flight hours to the site comptroller.

(c) Provide annual SBTP projection and monthly execution data per chapter 3.

5. Administration and Logistics. Standardization of Marine Corps flying hour reporting is essential to accurately track FHP execution, which is used for future FHP planning and programming decisions. The goal of standardized reporting is to accurately track execution of hours by training, support, operational, and contingency category. Additional report requirements may be requested via Naval message for tracking of FHP budget and execution (i.e. additional information to justify CPH variance).

a. Records Disposition. All FHP reports maintained by HQMC (APP-2) and MARFOR staff agencies shall be maintained for 10 years per reference (h) SSIC 3125.1.

b. Change Recommendations. Submit all recommendations concerning this Order to HQMC (APP-2) via the appropriate chain of command.

6. Commands and Signal

    a. Command. This Order is applicable to the Total Force Marine Corps.

    b. Signal. This Order is effective the date signed.

JAMES F. AMOS
Assistant Commandant
of the Marine Corps

DISTRIBUTION: PCN 10203181000

    Copy to: 7000260 (2)
              7000144/8145001 (1)

TABLE OF CONTENTS

Chapter 1

FHP OP-20 Display and Methodology Schedules

1. General. The FHP OP-20 display and main methodology categories are for: Tactical Aircraft; Fleet Air Training (FAT) OP-20 Methodology; Fleet Air Support (FAS) OP-20 Methodology, and Reserve Defined Methodology. The OP-20, see figure 2.1, is a Department of the Navy (DON) planning document published by OPNAV N43 for the FHP several times per year to establish the annual flying hours by Type/Model/Series (T/M/S), which is used for FHP funding and fleet planning. Requirements are computed by using the CCRM and revised with MARFOR input.

    a. Display. The OP-20 display and methodology schedules (not including Tactical Aircraft) are determined by the following standard criteria: FY; Schedule; COM/PAC/; T/M/S; Crew to seat ratio; crews; aircrew manning factor; budgeted crews; required hours/crew/mo; total hours required; total hours actual; actual cost per hour; total cost actual; actual hours/mo/crew and percent required hours funded. Additional information on OP-20 display is in the following paragraphs.

    b. Methodology. The OP-20 shows: required hours, budgeted hours, crew seat ratios, force structure, budgeted hours computed as a percentage of requirement; cost per hour by T/M/S; total costs by budget line item; and total T/M/S costs.

2. Specific Aircraft. Those aircraft, i.e., tactical, which serve a mission-essential function determined by the methodology described below. Tactical Aircraft (TACAIR) OP-20 Methodology, by year, schedule, LANT/PAC/Type/Model/Series (T/M/S):

    a. FY 2008 Final. Indicates the fiscal year of the display and the nature of the submission.

    b. Schedule "A", TACAIR/ASW. Indicates the purpose of the funding. In this case the funding is for the operation of TACAIR squadrons and the training of associated squadron, augment (staff), supervisory, and MAWTS crews.

    c. LANT. Indicates the claimant (command funded), in this case, MARFORCOM.

    d. (T/M/S). This column displays each aircraft by T/M/S for which funding has been budgeted.

    e. Forces. This figure is based on forces programmed in the Aircraft Program Data File (ADPF). Funding is based on Primary Mission Aircraft Authorized (PMAA) as reflected in that document. This number will be an average if the number of aircraft authorized changes during the fiscal year.

    f. Crew Seat Ratio. The crew seat ratio is computed by dividing T/O pilots by PMAA and multiplying by of .9, since funding is programmed for 90 percent of T/O.

    g. Crews. This number is computed by multiplying the number of aircraft times the crew seat ratio. This number should represent 90 percent of the T/O number of crews.

h. _Aircrew Manning Factor (AMF)_. It will be determined based on current actual manning. This number represents the current percentage of T/O that is actually manned. If actual manning is less than 100 percent of authorized, this number will be less than 1.000.

i. _Budgeted Crews_. This represents the number of aircrew funded.

j. _Req Hrs/Crew/Mo_. This number represents the total hours required per month to keep an aircrew core capable. These hourly requirements are determined by the CCRM, and include Training and Readiness (T&R) syllabus requirements.

k. _Total Hours Required_. This number is calculated by multiplying the number of crews, multiplied by the hours/crew/month, multiplied by 12.

l. _Total Hours Actual_. This number is a function of hours flown in the fiscal year.

m. _Actual Cost Per Hour (CPH)_. This number represents the total executed CPH and includes fuel CPH, maintenance CPH, Aviation Depot Level Repairable (AVDLR) CPH, and contract maintenance CPH.

n. _Total Cost Required_. This number is computed by multiplying the total hours required by the CPH.

o. _Total Cost Actual_. This number is computed by multiplying the total hours flown by the CPH.

p. _Actual Hours/Mo/Crew_. This figure represents the monthly execution of hours per crew for the fiscal year. It is computed by dividing actual hours by crews divided by 12.

q. _Percent Required Hours Funded_. This represents the percentage of total required hours funded. It is computed by dividing the total hours funded by total hours required and then multiplying by 100.

3. _Fleet Air Training (FAT) OP-20 Methodology_. The FHP OP-20 display and main methodology categories are for: Tactical Aircraft; Fleet Air Training (FAT) OP-20 Methodology; Fleet Air Support (FAS) OP-20 Methodology and Reserve Defined Methodology. OP-20 is a Department of the Navy (DON) planning document published by the OPNAV N43 for the Flying Hour Program (FHP) several times per year to establish the annual flying hours by Type/Model/Series, which is used for FHP funding and fleet planning. Requirements are computed by using the Core Competency Resource Model (CCRM) and revised with MARFORs.

a. _Display_. The OP-20 display and methodology schedules (not including Tactical Aircraft) are determined by the following standard criteria: FY; Schedule; LANT/PAC/; T/M/S; Crew to seat ratio; crews; aircrew manning factor; budgeted crews; req hours/crew/mo; total hours required; total hours actual; actual cost per hour; total cost actual; actual hours/mo/crew/ and percent required hours funded. Additional information is explained in the following paragraphs.

b. _Methodology_. The OP-20 shows: required hours, budgeted hours, crew seat ratios, force structure, budgeted hours computed as a percentage of requirement; cost per hour by T/M/S; total costs by budget line item; and total T/M/S costs.

4. Specific Training Criteria. Fleet Air Training (FAT) OP-20 Methodology is the following: FY; Schedule; T/M/S; number of aircraft; Categories: (I, II, III, IV, V); no PIL, Syllabus hours; pilot hours; no Naval Flight Officer(s); syllabus hours; NFO hours; task hours; total hours required; total hours budgeted; budgeted cost per hour; total cost required; in millions required; and percent required hours funded.

a. FY 2008 Budgeted. Indicates the fiscal year of the display and the nature of the submission.

b. Schedule "B", 1A2A. Indicates the purpose of the funding. In this case the funding is for the operation of FRS squadrons and the training of associated squadron students.

c. T/M/S. This column displays each aircraft by T/M/S for which funding has been budgeted.

d. Forces. This figure is based on forces programmed in the APDF. Funding is based on PMAA as reflected in that document. This number will be an average if the number of aircraft authorized changes during the fiscal year.

e. Category (CAT). This represents the number of students within each type of syllabus.

f. CAT I. First Tour Aviator or First Tour in Type (Warfare Transition). Receives 100 percent of Syllabus. For USMC, this equates to the basic transition Programs of Instruction (POIs).

g. Second Tour in Type Aircraft. Receives approximately 75 percent of CAT I Syllabus. For USMC this equates to the Conversion POI.

h. Third Tour (Commanding Officer or Executive Officer). Receives approximately 50 percent of CAT I syllabus. (For transition pilots, the need and/or length of the FRS syllabus depends on the complexity of either the weapons systems and/or the flight characteristics of the type aircraft to which they are transitioning). For USMC, this equates to the Refresher POI.

i. CAT IV. Typically, a Naval Aviation Training and Operating Procedures Standardization (NATOPS) check or enough training to safely operate the aircraft without supervision. Receives about 10-20 percent of the CAT I syllabus. For USMC, this equates to a Modified Refresher Program.

j. CAT V. A specialized syllabus that does not meet the criteria of the first four categories. Other POIs not described above.

k. Number of Pilots. This number represents the pilot throughput for the current fiscal year. Estimated number of pilots who will complete the syllabus.

l. Syllabus Hours. The number of hours required to complete the syllabus for a particular category.

m. Pilot Hours. This number is computed by multiplying the pilot throughput by the syllabus hours.

n. Number of Naval Flight Officer(s) (NFO). This number represents the NFO throughput for the current fiscal year. Estimated number of NFOs who will complete the syllabus.

o. <u>Syllabus Hours</u>. The number of hours required to complete the syllabus for a particular category.

p. <u>NFO Hours</u>. This number is computed by multiplying the NFO throughput by the syllabus hours.

q. <u>Task Hours</u>. Those hours unrelated to a specific syllabus.

r. <u>Total Hours Required</u>. This number is calculated by adding the pilot hours, NFO hours, and Task hours.

s. <u>Total Hours Budgeted</u>. This number represents the number of hours programmed for the current fiscal year.

t. <u>Budgeted Cost Per Hour</u>. This number represents the total budgeted CPH and includes fuel CPH, maintenance CPH, AVDLR CPH, and contract maintenance CPH.

u. <u>Total Cost Required</u>. This number is computed by multiplying the total hours required by the CPH.

v. <u>In Millions Budgeted</u>. This number is computed by multiplying the programmed hours by the CPH.

w. <u>Percent Required Hrs Funded</u>. This is the percentage of total required hours funded. It is computed by dividing the total hours funded by total hours required, and then multiplying by 100.

5. <u>Fleet Air Support (FAS) OP-20 Methodology</u>. The FHP OP-20 display and main methodology categories are for: Tactical Aircraft; Fleet Air Training (FAT) OP-20 Methodology; Fleet Air Support (FAS) OP-20 Methodology and Reserve Defined Methodology. OP-20 is a Department of the Navy (DON) planning document published by the OPNAV N43 for the Flying Hour Program (FHP) several times per year to establish the annual flying hours by Type/Model/Series, which is used for FHP funding and fleet planning. Requirements are computed by using the Core Competency Resource Model (CCRM) and revised with MARFOR (Commander, Marine Forces Reserve) inputs.

a. <u>Display</u>. The OP-20 display and methodology schedules (not including Tactical Aircraft) are determined by the following standard criteria: FY; Schedule; T/M/S; UTIL, number of aircraft; budgeted cost per hour; total hours required; total costs required; total hours budgeted; total costs budgeted; and percent required hours funded. Additional information is explained in the following paragraphs.

b. <u>Methodology</u>. Fleet Air Support Reserve Manpower Criteria determined by the methodology described below.

(1) <u>FY 2008 Budgeted</u>. Indicates the fiscal year of the display and the nature of the submission.

(2) <u>Schedule "C", 1A1A</u>. Indicates the purpose of the funding. In this case the funding is for the operation of FAS squadrons and the training of associated squadron pilots.

(3) <u>T/M/S</u>. This column displays each aircraft by T/M/S for which funding has been budgeted.

(4) <u>UTIL</u>. This column displays the number hours executed per aircraft per month.

(5) <u>Forces</u>. This figure is based on forces programmed in the APDF. Funding is based on PMAA as reflected in that document. This number will be an average if the number of aircraft authorized changes during the FY.

(6) <u>Budgeted Cost Per Hour</u>. This number represents the total budgeted CPH and includes fuel CPH, maintenance CPH, AVDLR CPH, and contract maintenance CPH.

(7) <u>Total Hours Required</u>. This number is calculated by using historical logistics and support execution and known training requirements.

(8) <u>Total Costs Required</u>. This number is computed by multiplying the total hours required by the CPH.

(9) <u>Total Hours Budgeted</u>. This number represents the number of hours programmed for the current fiscal year.

(10) <u>Total Costs Budgeted</u>. This number is computed by multiplying the programmed hours by the CPH.

(11) <u>Percent Required Hours Funded</u>. This represents the percentage of total required hours funded. It is computed by dividing the total hours funded by total hours required and then multiplying by 100.

6. <u>Reserve Defined Methodology</u>. The FHP OP-20 display and main methodology categories are for: Tactical Aircraft; Fleet Air Training (FAT) OP-20 Methodology; Fleet Air Support (FAS) OP-20 Methodology and Reserve Defined Methodology hours budgeted; total costs budgeted; and percent required hours funded. Additional information is explained in the following paragraphs.

a. <u>Display</u>. OP-20 is a Department of the Navy (DON) planning document published by the OPNAV N43 for the Flying Hour Program (FHP) several times per year to establish the annual flying hours by Type/Model/Series, which is used for FHP funding and fleet planning. Requirements are computed by using the Core Competency Resource Model (CCRM) and revised with MARFOR (Commander, Marine Forces Reserve) inputs.

b. <u>Methodology</u>. The OP-20 display and methodology schedules (not including Tactical Aircraft) are determined by the following standard criteria: FY; schedule; UTIL; Number of aircraft; budgeted cost per hour; total hours required; total costs budgeted; and percent required hours funded.

(1) <u>FY 2008 Budgeted</u>. Indicates the FY of the display and the nature of the submission.

(2) <u>Schedule "D", 1A1A</u>. Indicates the purpose of the funding. In this case the funding is for the operation of Reserve squadrons and the training of associated squadron pilots.

(3) <u>T/M/S</u>. This column displays each aircraft by T/M/S for which funding has been budgeted.

(4) <u>UTIL</u>. This column displays the number hours executed per aircraft per month.

(5) <u>Forces</u>. This figure is based on forces programmed in the APDF. Funding is based on PMAA as reflected in that document. This number will be an average if the number of aircraft authorized changes during the FY.

(6) <u>Budgeted Cost Per Hour</u>. This number represents the total budgeted CPH and includes fuel CPH, maintenance CPH, AVDLR CPH, and contract maintenance CPH.

(7) <u>Total Hours Required</u>. This number is calculated by using historical logistics and support execution and known training requirements.

(8) <u>Total Costs Required</u>. This number is computed by multiplying the total hours required by the CPH.

(9) <u>Total Hours Budgeted</u>. This number represents the number of hours programmed for the current fiscal year.

(10) <u>Total Costs Budgeted</u>. This number is computed by multiplying the programmed hours by the CPH.

(11) <u>Percent Required Hours Funded</u>. This is the percentage of total required hours funded. It is computed by dividing the total hours funded by total hours required and then multiplying by 100.

UNCLASSIFIED
U. S. ATLANTIC FLEET
FY: 2008

Department of the Navy OP-20
Analysis of Navy Flying Budget BackUp Exhibit

Page 1 of 23
01/03/2008

Version: 2061 09- -97 -PB (PRESIDENTIAL BUDGET)

GEN PURPOSE FORCES

Program Element	TMS	Forces	Util	Hours	FF/Fuel	FA/DLR	FM/Maint	FW/CONTRACT	FO/OTHER	ADJ	Total	Hrly Fuel Cons Rate
					Cost Per Hour / Annual Cost, in Millions							
02 06110 M	AV-8B	42.0	21.054	10611	1809.25	4717.18	1377.25	0.00	0.00	0.00	7903.68	19.670
					19.198	50.054	14.614	0.000	0.000	0.000	83.866	
PE 0206110M TOTAL:		**42.0**	**21.054**	**10611**	**1809.25**	**4717.18**	**1377.25**	**0.00**	**0.00**	**0.00**	**7903.68**	**19.670**
					19.198	**50.054**	**14.614**	**0.000**	**0.000**	**0.000**	**83.866**	
02 06121 M	CH-46E	48.0	11.762	6775	418.51	3175.69	1284.10	0.00	0.00	0.00	4878.30	4.550
					2.835	21.515	8.700	0.000	0.000	0.000	33.050	
	MV-22B	24.0	29.538	8507	1202.18	77.06	447.94	0.00	0.00	0.00	1727.18	13.070
					10.227	0.656	3.811	0.000	0.000	0.000	14.693	
PE 0206121M TOTAL:		**72.0**	**17.688**	**15282**	**854.75**	**1450.78**	**818.64**	**0.00**	**0.00**	**0.00**	**3124.17**	**9.293**
					13.062	**22.171**	**12.510**	**0.000**	**0.000**	**0.000**	**47.744**	
02 06122 M	CH-53E	40.0	17.913	8598	1010.22	7825.98	2136.68	0.00	0.00	0.00	10972.88	10.983
					8.686	67.288	18.371	0.000	0.000	0.000	94.345	
PE 0206122M TOTAL:		**40.0**	**17.913**	**8598**	**1010.22**	**7825.98**	**2136.68**	**0.00**	**0.00**	**0.00**	**10972.88**	**10.983**
					8.686	**67.288**	**18.371**	**0.000**	**0.000**	**0.000**	**94.345**	
02 06127 M	KC-130J	12.0	36.125	5202	1476.37	302.29	204.22	0.00	0.00	0.00	1982.88	16.051
					7.680	1.573	1.062	0.000	0.000	0.000	10.315	
PE 0206127M TOTAL:		**12.0**	**36.125**	**5202**	**1476.37**	**302.29**	**204.22**	**0.00**	**0.00**	**0.00**	**1982.88**	**16.051**
					7.680	**1.573**	**1.062**	**0.000**	**0.000**	**0.000**	**10.315**	
02 06131 M	AH-1W	42.0	17.982	9063	220.84	3186.36	1331.86	0.00	0.00	0.00	4739.06	2.401
					2.001	28.878	12.071	0.000	0.000	0.000	42.950	
	UH-1N	21.0	19.714	4968	215.88	1494.11	1389.21	0.00	0.00	0.00	3099.20	2.347
					1.072	7.423	6.902	0.000	0.000	0.000	15.397	
PE 0206131M TOTAL:		**63.0**	**18.560**	**14031**	**219.08**	**2587.18**	**1352.17**	**0.00**	**0.00**	**0.00**	**4158.43**	**2.382**
					3.074	**36.301**	**18.972**	**0.000**	**0.000**	**0.000**	**58.347**	
02 06134 M	FA-18A	24.0	24.896	7170	2340.89	3312.42	1387.75	0.00	0.00	0.00	7041.06	25.450
					16.784	23.750	9.950	0.000	0.000	0.000	50.484	
	FA-18C	24.0	24.896	7170	2385.96	2813.48	1821.05	0.00	0.00	0.00	7020.49	25.940
					17.107	20.173	13.057	0.000	0.000	0.000	50.337	
	FA-18D	24.0	26.378	7597	2525.49	3274.65	1256.41	0.00	0.00	0.00	7056.55	27.457
					19.186	24.878	9.545	0.000	0.000	0.000	53.609	
PE 0206134M TOTAL:		**72.0**	**25.390**	**21937**	**2419.55**	**3136.26**	**1483.89**	**0.00**	**0.00**	**0.00**	**7039.70**	**26.305**
					53.078	**68.800**	**32.552**	**0.000**	**0.000**	**0.000**	**154.430**	

Figure 1-1. -- Department of the Navy OP-20 Display Analysis of Navy Flying Budget BackUp Exhibit

Chapter 2

Core Competency Resource Model Guidelines

1. General

    a. In 1997, the Marine Corps introduced the Marine Aviation Campaign Plan (MACP), and with it, the Sortie Based Training Program (SBTP). The intent was to evolve from a process where readiness is measured purely in terms of hours flown to one where readiness is based upon the actual training achievements of the sortie. Using the specific Type/Model/Series (T/M/S) T&R requirements as the guide, the training achievements of a sortie can be directly measured in terms of their success in meeting Training and Readiness (T&R) goals. Taken collectively, a squadron's historical execution of T&R-coded sorties builds a picture of that squadron's readiness as defined by its own T&R. This is done by measuring Core Skill Proficiency, Combat Leadership, Instructor Training, and other specific Requirements, Qualifications and Designations delineated in the individual T/M/S T&Rs. In order to accurately determine its annual flight hour requirement for training, and the monetary resources necessary to meet that requirement, the Marine Corps developed the Core Competency Resource Model (CCRM). This model ensures adequate funding for the future needs of the USMC FHP by quantifying the peacetime training requirements for each T/M/S T&R.

    b. The CCRM links every T&R sortie to unit readiness, which is defined by core proficiencies that are stated in each T&R Manual. In essence, the CCRM calculates a generic squadron's flight hour requirements, directly linking the FHP, T&R syllabi, and readiness reporting (SORTS/DRRS, CMTR and M-SHARP), as was directed per the MACP. Specifically, the CCRM, which has been accredited and validated by the Chief of Naval Operations (CNO) and Commandant of the Marine Corps (CMC), generates annual flight hour and sortie requirements (broken down by training, support, and operational sorties) for maintaining selected T-Level readiness ratings. DC AVN (APP) utilizes this CCRM data as the primary validation tool when providing input to the Navy's budgeting document, known as the OP-20. Operational units may use the CCRM output as a resource to help develop their own annual flying hour plan, although it is not meant to be a squadron commander's sole tool for determining the squadron's annual flight hour requirement. DC AVN is the advocate for the CCRM and oversees its implementation, while Training and Education Command's (TECOM) Aviation Training Branch (ATB) is the custodian of the model, ensuring its accuracy and alignment with current T&R manuals. The most current CCRM and its applicable operating directions are available on the TECOM website at http://www.tecom.usmc.mil/atb/ccrm. When using the CCRM, it is imperative that operational planners ensure they have the most current model (by comparing the date of the CCRM with the latest syllabus date), since T&R manuals often change and the sortie requirement that populates the model changes concurrently. Inputs may be made on the website and outputs are immediately given. Saving the data as a file disables the functionality of the website, but does provide a screenshot of the final input and output.

2. CCRM Uses

    a. Headquarters. The CCRM produces a notional squadron's annual flight hour requirement according to the T/M/S' T&R training requirements and individual breakdown of its aircrew. The primary inputs to the CCRM are: 1) current T/M/S T & R Manuals, 2) average sortie duration, 3) projected number and type of fleet aircrew (basic, refresher, maintain syllabus etc). The average sortie durations are listed in reference (c). This average sortie length is applied to all of the sorties in the model, and it represents an average of the mix of various sortie lengths from historical T/M/S execution. The T&R standards are only changed through a conference, so the most dynamic and key element is the number and type of aircrew. HQMC uses the CCRM to create rough requirements, or "benchmarks," for each T/M/S; in other words, a flight hour requirement for a generic squadron (manned with a standard number and type of aircrew equal to 90% of the squadron's T/O for aircrew) within each T/M/S. This benchmark is not necessarily the correct flight hour requirement for each squadron within that particular T/M/S, but in aggregate, it provides a realistic requirement for each T/M/S. By multiplying the CCRM output by the number of squadrons flying that specific T/M/S, HQMC can provide the annual training requirement to the DON programming and budgeting offices in order to ensure that the entire USMC FHP is funded at an appropriate level.

b. Fleet Operational Planners. The CCRM provides one of many tools available to operations officers to use when developing SBTPs; however, it does not take the place of proper operational planning and sortie management. The primary input for squadron operations officers is the number and type of aircrew (basic, refresher, maintain syllabus). It is incumbent upon each unit to input their current and projected number of crews, averaged through the entire year, to give them a rough flight hour requirement particular to their unit. The CCRM provides a starting point for operational planners to deviate from in determining their total annual requirement, and it is up to each unit to tailor this requirement to their individual personnel breakdown and training requirements. Operational planners must take into account all factors that affect training in order to develop a monthly SBTP that is realistic and executable, while striving to meet readiness goals. Most operational planners will find that their specific squadron will require either more or fewer sorties and hours than would be required by the CCRM due to their unique situation. Factors that will affect a squadron's sortie and flight hour planning include (but are not limited to):

(1) Type and number of aircrew that are part of, or will be part of, the squadron.

(2) Squadron TEEP and the sorties needed to execute the travel to, from, and during deployed and detachment operations. Deployments in support of GWOT may require that certain Core Skills in the T&R Manual require more sorties than the refly calls for, or an "Operational Focus," while other Core Skills may temporarily be allowed to fall out of currency until the contingency deployment is complete.

(3) Availability of aircraft, simulators, ranges, ordnance and other training resources used in T&R events. Planned maintenance days and traditionally active periods of inclement weather can be planned for based on historical experience.

(4) Squadron Training Plans, including Instructor work-ups, Qualifications, and Designations.

(5) Functional Test Flights, test sorties and ferry flights.

(6) Special events that affect flight scheduling such as Changes of Command, holidays and mandatory technical or ground training for aircrew and maintenance Marines.

(7) Expected fragged events and support flight requirements.

(8) Different sortie lengths based upon different training phases, and the availability of tankers and hot-pits for scheduling.

3. CCRM Inputs

a. Primary unit-level inputs are in the manning input section (lower left green portion of the main page). See Figure 32-1. Primary outputs are the numbers of sorties, flight hours, sorties per crew per month and hours per crew per month (H/C/M) required to maintain a specific training level (T-1 through T-4, which are located on the upper left portion of the page in blue, green yellow and red).

b. Operational planners can input their squadron aircrew makeup (number of basics, refresh, maintain syllabus etc). This is essential since the flight hour requirement for a "basic" (new aircrew) is larger than the flight hour requirement for a "maintain" (regular squadron aircrew) or a "refresher" syllabus.

c. The total number of aircrew should be the average of what a unit expects to have over the course of the year. Obviously, no squadron can completely predict its manning levels or who exactly will join or leave the squadron, but a best guess based upon MAG and squadron personnel planning is appropriate and applicable in determining the squadron's aircrew numbers.

Aircrew Categories:

Basic- New pilot responsible for flying the entire syllabus.

Refresher- Returning aircrew responsible for flying the R-coded portion of the syllabus.

Maintain- Everyday squadron aircrew, responsible for flying the maintain syllabus within the appropriate refly intervals.

Augment- Aircrew working in temporary staff billets that the squadron plans to take to war with them, fly the maintain syllabus. Does not apply to all T/M/S.

Staff- Aircrew in permanent staff positions assigned by the MAW to fly with the squadron.

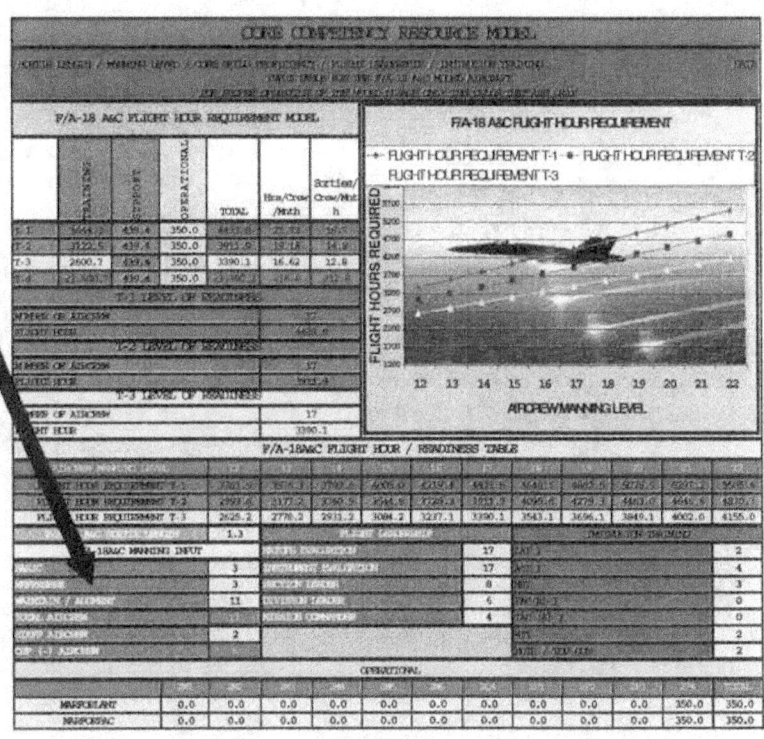

Figure 2-1. -- CCRM User Interface Page

d. Projected number of Instructor Training and other specific Requirements, Qualifications and Designations, input by operational planner at the bottom of the page. The model will calculate a number of sorties and hours to correspond with all of the T&R requirements to build a new Instructor, Qualification or Designation.

e. Expected Operational Hours are located at the bottom of the model in grey. Utilizing historical information from NALCOMIS/SARA/M-SHARP, and including known TEEP operational commitments, the planner can change the expected Operational Flight Hour requirement. The number that is currently in the model is an historical squadron average based upon the T/M/S' last five years' of execution data.

    f. The CCRM produces an annual squadron flight hour requirement for different training levels. The Marine Corps FHP is funded to support the flight hour requirement that equates to a readiness of T-2. For operational planners, this is the level of readiness that ensures a squadron is prepared to deploy and can meet all required mission areas at the required level and tempo. Although the CCRM provides the annual hour and sortie requirement, a monthly breakdown of flight hours and H/C/M particular to each individual unit should be produced as part of a SBTP per enclosure chapter (56).

4. <u>CCRM Terms of Reference</u>. The following are terms of reference that are essential to understanding the CCRM, its integration with the T&R Manual, FHP, and SBTP as well as its tie to unit level readiness.

    a. <u>Mission Essential Task List (METL)</u>. The unit METL is a standardized list of tasks a unit must be able to accomplish during combat/contingency operations.

    b. <u>Core Capability</u>. A standardized measure of performance that a Marine Air Ground Task Force commander should expect during sustained contingency/combat operations. Combat flight operations define core capability in terms of a daily-sustained sortie rate, or operational coverage, in support of a METL.

    c. <u>Combat Leadership</u>. Unit competency in leadership is defined in terms of minimum numbers of required tactical leaders certified per T&R standard and designated by the unit commanding officer.

    d. <u>Core Skill Proficiency (CSP)</u>. The number of individuals, or crews, required to be proficient in each core skill. An individual is considered CSP when they have completed, and maintain currency in, the requisite T&R syllabus for that particular skill.

    e. <u>Core Model Minimum Requirement (CMMR)</u>. The minimum number of crews necessary in each particular core skill for a unit to accomplish its mission and METLs. CMMR and flight leadership requirements are the foundation of a unit's SBTP and flying hour requirement, as well its direct tie to unit T-Level readiness.

Chapter 3

<u>Marine Corps Sortie Based Training Program (SBTP)</u>

1. <u>General</u>. The Marine Corps SBTP allows squadron commanders to develop an annual SBTP that reflects their unit's Training Exercise Employment Plan (TEEP) and unit Training and Readiness (T&R)' requirements to train mission skill proficient aircrews and flight leads per their unit T&R Core Model Minimum Requirement (CMMR) to attain and maintain a T-2 level of readiness per reference (c). A T-2 level of readiness allows a unit to fulfill its Mission Essential Task output standard in support of a Marine Air Ground Task Force or Joint Force Commander.

    a. <u>Participation</u>. All active and reserve Marine Corps flying squadrons shall participate in the SBTP, including tactical fleet squadrons, Fleet Replacement Squadrons (FRSs), and Operational Support Aircraft (OSA) activities, with the exception of HMX-1, MAWTS-1, and VMFAT-101. The unique nature and mission of FRS and OSA activities may prevent those units from meeting or sustaining CMMR requirements. However, their participation in the SBTP is necessary to provide DC AVN and resource planners the data required to support accurate FHP budget allocations.

    b. <u>Scope</u>. The SBTP manages forecast and execution flight hours and sorties for each Type/Model/Series (T/M/S) the squadron operates. In addition, the SBTP manages core skills, mission skills, and flight leadership data for crewmembers in each T&R syllabus associated with those TMSs including pilots, Naval Flight Officers (NFOs), and enlisted aircrew. For example, in an HMLA squadron, SBTP manages AH-1W and UH-1N flight hours and sorties, as well as information about AH-1W Pilots, UH-1N Pilots, UH-1N Crew Chiefs, and UH-1N Aerial Observer/Gunners. Some T/M/Ss are grouped together for SBTP reporting in order to align the structure of T/M/S T&R manuals. The KC-130 F, R, and T are grouped together as one T/M/S group, but the KC-130J is separate. The F/A-18 A and C are grouped together, but the F/A-18D is separate. The CH-53 D and E are treated separately as are the AH-1W, AH-1Z, UH-1N and UH-1Y.

    c. <u>M-SHARP</u>. The Marine Corps Sierra-Hotel Aviation Readiness Program (M-SHARP) is the automated system used throughout Marine Aviation to manage the Training and Readiness (T&R) program per NAVMC 3500.14 and is the authoritative data source for documenting all Marine Corps aviation flight records (NAVFLIRs), aircrew T&R data, and readiness reporting as required. M-SHARP is also the management tool for the Sortie Based Training Program (SBTP).

2. <u>SBTP Reporting</u>. There are two Marine aviation SBTP reporting requirements; the Annual Unit SBTP Forecast submission, and the Monthly SBTP Execution Report.

    a. <u>Annual Unit SBTP Forecast</u>. The annual unit SBTP forecast is developed at the squadron level, then reviewed and approved by the Marine Aircraft Group (MAG)/Marine Aircraft Wing (MAW)/Marine Corps Installations (MCI)/Marine Force (MARFOR)/DC AVN chain of command. DC AVN (APP-2) consolidates the MARFOR T/M/S inputs into a single Marine Aviation SBTP by T/M/S. Unit SBTP Forecasts shall be submitted by squadrons NLT 01 August each year for the following fiscal year (FY). DC AVN (APP-2) utilizes the T&R T/M/S Core Competency Resource Models (CCRM) and the MARFOR T/M/S SBTP submissions for the final development of the Marine aviation Tactical

Aircraft (TACAIR) Flying Hour Program (FHP) requirement for DC AVN approval prior to submission to OPNAV N43.

(1) Unit CCRM, TEEP, SBTP Interface. Unit commanders may utilize the appropriate T/M/S CCRM to help determine annual sorties and flight hours required per the unit's projected aircrew (basic, refresher, maintain, augment, staff) assignments. Each unit will have a unique CCRM requirement and TEEP that provides the initial input during the development of the annual unit SBTP sortie and FHP requirement. The CCRM represents a starting point for the unit and the following represents a squadron operational planner's guidelines for developing an accurate, executable flying hour plan:

(a) Type and number of aircrew present or projected to join the squadron.

(b) Squadron TEEP and the sorties needed to travel to, from, and during deployment or detachment operations. Deployments in support of Global War on Terrorism (GWOT) (or other contingencies) may require greater precision in certain mission skill sets (i.e. ordnance delivery in urban environments) and necessitate more sorties to refine these mission skills than the T&R dictates. Other mission skills may be allowed to expire temporarily until the contingency deployment is complete.

(c) Availability of aircraft, simulators, ranges, ordnance and other training resources used in T&R events. Planned maintenance days and traditional periods of inclement weather can be planned for based on historical data.

(d) Squadron Training Plans, including Instructor work-ups, Qualifications, and Designations.

(e) Functional Test Flights, test sorties and ferry flights.

(f) Special events that affect flight scheduling such as Changes of Command, holidays and mandatory technical or ground training for aircrew and maintenance Marines.

(g) Expected fragged events and support flight requirements.

(h) Different sortie lengths based upon different training phases, and the availability of tankers and hot-pits for scheduling.

(2) SBTP, OP-20 Reconciliation. During the approval process, operations/G-3 departments at all levels must reconcile their subordinate commands' SBTP inputs against projected flight hour controls in the OP-20 in order to ensure that flight hour allocations match priorities and remain within fiscal constraints. Once validated by the MARFOR and forwarded to DC (AVN), the SBTP defines the flight hour goal for a squadron. While deviations from the plan on a month-to-month basis will be unavoidable as the TEEP and squadron composition change, squadrons should try to meet their quarterly totals and ensure their MAG/HHQ is aware of potential shortcomings or overages in flight hour execution. Deviations from projected delivery schedules of replacement aircrew may force a unit to substantially shift flight hours to accommodate late arrivals. Revised flight hour consumption to accommodate personnel sourcing must be coordinated with the MAG and closely monitored by the Wing to ensure resources are adequately re-allocated prior to the close of the Fiscal Year. Only the MAG (with the Wing and MARFOR concurrence) or MCI (with MARFOR concurrence) can re-allocate hours to different units or T/M/S. MAGs, Wings and MCIs will not alter their annual

total without MARFOR approval, with notice to HQMC AVN as this occurs. To help streamline this process, an annual mid-year review will be conducted by the MARFORs in order to ensure that flight hour allocations are matched with priorities and remain within budget constraints. Changes to the SBTP as a result of mid-year review must be coordinated with HQMC and USFF (if needed).

(3) Contingency Operations. For units scheduled to deploy to known contingency operations during the upcoming FY, the sorties and flight hours forecast for those months should not drastically exceed a notional peacetime deployment flight hour profile. This is because the SBTP is a tool for measuring training and qualification levels within a unit. Contingency hours flown in excess of the SBTP FHP are covered via supplemental funding and defined as incremental contingency hours. Squadrons report total contingency hours on their SBTP and budget OPTAR reports. Most importantly, MARFORs should provide guidance to deploying units for the number of hours they should forecast when deploying in support of a contingency operation. Incremental contingency hours in excess of forecast hours will be calculated in accordance with reference (a) and chapter 4 of this Order.

(4) M-SHARP Procedures for SBTP Forecast Submission. Squadrons will use M-SHARP to enter and submit their annual SBTP forecast and the chain of command will use M-SHARP to review/approve squadron SBTP forecasts.

(a) Submit Procedures. Participating squadrons may edit and save the SBTP forecast as frequently as needed until the forecast is submitted. Squadrons will submit their forecast by selecting the "Submit" button on the SBTP Forecast page in the M-SHARP Setup module. Once submitted, squadrons will be unable to modify their SBTP forecast unless it is unsubmitted by a senior command, generally the MAG or higher. Senior commands will then review subordinate squadron annual SBTP forecast submissions. Note: SBTP forecasts are not routed to each level of the chain of command separately. The data is made available to all senior commands simultaneously. Therefore, only squadrons will have the authority to submit a SBTP Forecast in M-SHARP in order to prevent a senior command from modifying a submission without the squadron's knowledge.

(b) Unsubmit Procedures. Once a squadron's SBTP forecast is submitted, no command is able to edit it unless the forecast is unsubmitted by selecting the "Unsubmit" button on the SBTP Forecast page in the M-SHARP Setup module. While reviewing the SBTP forecasts, any senior command may unsubmit a squadron's forecast then coordinate modifications needed via normal communication channels with the squadron (phone, email, etc). Only MAGs and above will have the authority to unsubmit a forecast in order to prevent a squadron from modifying a previously-submitted forecast without the chain of command's knowledge. All editing of SBTP forecasts will occur at the squadron level. It is inappropriate for a single command or person to have both submission and unsubmission authority.

b. Monthly Unit SBTP Execution Report. The monthly unit SBTP execution report has two distinct purposes. First, it provides squadrons and above the data required to track unit SBTP and FHP execution. Second, it provides HQMC the standardized T/M/S Marine Aviation Readiness metrics for the Marine Corps Current Readiness Assessment System (MCCRATS) under the Naval Aviation Enterprise (NAE).

(1) The M-SHARP Procedures for Monthly Unit SBTP Reports is t. The monthly SBTP Execution Report, which contains the squadrons' forecast and execution data together, is drawn directly from squadron M-SHARP databases with no action required by squadrons except initial data setup/baselining and

annual SBTP forecast submission. Deployed units using the M-SHARP Deployable installation will continue to participate in the SBTP provided they submit M-SHARP Synchronization of Portable Installation (SPIN) files per reference (o). SPIN files automatically populate the global M-SHARP database with data required by the SBTP. There are no submit/unsubmit procedures for the monthly SBTP Execution Report. SBTP Execution Reports are accessible in M-SHARP to designated squadron personnel and key individuals at each unit in the chain of command.

3. Flight Hour/Sortie Calculations. For SBTP purposes, it is necessary to specify the means by which flight hours and sorties are derived in order for commanders to make accurate forecast projections.

a. USMC Sortie Definition Standardization. It is imperative that all Flying Squadrons have a single definition of a USMC sortie if Marine Aviation is going to accurately plan and report the SBTP and FHP. The definition of a USMC Sortie is identical to the definition of a Flight, in accordance with reference (e): "For operational purposes, a flight is one or more aircraft proceeding on a common mission. For recording and reporting purposes, a flight begins when the aircraft first moves forward on its takeoff run or takes off vertically from rest at any point of support and ends after airborne flight when the aircraft is on the surface and either: a) the engines are stopped or the aircraft has been on the surface for 5 minutes, whichever comes first, b) a change is made by the pilot in command. For helicopters, a flight begins when the aircraft lifts from a rest point or commences ground taxi and ends after airborne flight when the rotors are disengaged or the aircraft has been stationary for 5 minutes with rotors engaged." Essentially, the number of sorties will equal the number of legs recorded on the Naval Aviation Flight Record (NAVFLIR) and is not directly linked to number of flight hours or T&R codes completed. The following are some examples of both fixed wing and rotary wing sorties:

(1) Example #1, Fixed-Wing Sortie. A single F/A-18 departs NBC for G-10 on a Close Air Support mission in support of ground units. The aircraft drops ordnance at G-10 and then flies to NKT and hot refuels in 15 minutes. After refueling, the aircraft returns to G-10 and drops a different type of ordnance and then flies to NBC and lands, mission complete. This event would be 2 sorties and logged as 2 legs on a single NAVFLIR.

(2) Example #2, Fixed-Wing Sortie. A single KC-130 departs NKX for the training area. Once in the training area the aircraft aerial refuels (AR) a section of F/A-18s and then aerial refuels a section of CH-53s. Upon AR completion, the aircraft returns to NKX and completes an annual pilot instrument check. This event would be 1 sortie and logged as 1 leg on a single NAVFLIR.

(3) Example #3, Rotary-Wing Sortie. A section of AH-1s departs Camp Pendleton and flies to Twenty-nine Palms, lands and hot refuels, spending 7 minutes on the deck. Then the aircraft fly CAS ISO ground units, lands and hot refuels again at NXP spending 10 minutes on the deck. After the second hot refuel, the aircraft flies to NFG and lands mission complete. This event would be a total of 6 sorties: 1 NAVFLIR for each aircraft, each NAVFLIR with 3 legs.

(4) Example #4, Rotary-Wing Sortie. A single CH-46 departs NCA and flies to Camp Lejeune for two ground troop inserts. The first insert requires 6 minutes on the ground to load troops and only 2 minutes in the zone to unload troops before returning for the second insert which follows the same timeline. After unloading troops for the second insert, the aircraft then

flies to NCA and hot refuels spending 8 minutes on the deck. After refueling, the aircraft flies a NATOPS check at NCA and then lands mission complete at NCA. This event would be 4 sorties and logged as 4 legs on a single NAVFLIR.

b. <u>SBTP Flight Hour Categories</u>. The SBTP and FHP require executed flight hours to be accurately tracked within 4 specific categories: Training, Support, Operational, and Contingency. These SBTP Flight Hour Categories are captured directly by M-SHARP and are no longer associated with or derived from Total Mission Requirement (TMR) codes. Aircrew shall attribute all flight time to one or more of these categories.

(1) <u>Training Hours</u>. Includes all flight training in accordance with T/M/S T&R manuals (initial or refly), flight leadership, and OPNAV-directed instrument training minimums. Whenever any member of the crew is receiving either an initial T&R credit or an update of a T&R code, they should log training hours specifically for the training portion of the sortie, including when participating in a frag or other operational sortie. The key difference between a training and operational sortie is if any member of the flight is able to log a T&R code, whether it is initial or refly, that portion of the sortie is logged as training. The remaining portion of the flight, including the transit, is logged as operational time to capture the external requirements imposed on fleet units. The only exception is for sorties flown in support of a contingency or combat operation, in which case they should be considered contingency hours. Note that any dedicated training flight that is aborted in-flight or is incomplete for any reason shall be attributed to support hours.

(2) <u>Support Hours</u>. Includes all squadron-generated sorties that do not fit the criteria for training and are not specifically tasked by an outside command or agency. Specific examples include FCFs, FCP under training, instructor under training (IUT), flights conducted at MAWTS-1 during a Weapons and Tactics Instructor Course, and non-training ferry/transit flights. Any dedicated training flight that is aborted in-flight or is incomplete for any reason shall be attributed to support hours.

(3) <u>Operational Hours</u>. Includes all squadron-generated sorties that do not fit the criteria for training and are specifically tasked by an outside command or agency. If aircrew T&R syllabus training is conducted in accordance with operational flights, log any non-T&R producing time as operational once T&R requirements have been satisfied or if there is significant non-T&R transit or loiter time involved.

(4) <u>Contingency Hours</u>. Includes all sorties flown in support of a contingency or combat operation, whether or not a T&R code can be logged. Assault support aircraft operating in geographic areas formally designated as contingency should log contingency hours for every flight in support of that contingency.

c. <u>Aircraft Unit Assignments</u>. Flight hours and sorties flown by an individual aircraft are always attributed to the unit that owns the aircraft in NALCOMIS/M-SHARP and NOT by the unit to which the personnel in that aircraft are assigned. Therefore, if crewmembers from Squadron A use an aircraft from Squadron B (without conducting a transfer of that aircraft to Squadron A), all hours and sorties logged by Squadron A crew are attributed to Squadron B for all budgeting, accounting, and SBTP purposes.

d. <u>Flight Simulator Usage</u>. All simulator flight events must be recorded in M-SHARP to enable higher headquarters to accurately track simulator usage and the contribution to training readiness that flight simulators provide. Flight time logged in simulators is always attributed to the unit to which the personnel on the simulator event are assigned.

4. <u>SBTP Responsibilities</u>. The execution of the Marine Corps SBTP requires the following assignment of responsibilities.

    a. <u>DC AVN (APP-2)</u>

        (1) <u>Annual Unit SBTP Forecast Submission</u>. Consolidate all SBTP Forecasts electronically no earlier than 23 August and develop the Marine Aviation Sortie Based Training Plan Forecast for DC AVN.

        (2) <u>Monthly Unit SBTP Execution Reporting</u>. Consolidate squadron execution reports by T/M/S electronically no earlier than the 6th working day of the following month and develop the Marine Aviation Sortie Based Training Plan Execution Update for DC AVN.

    b. <u>MARFORCOM, MARFORPAC, and MARFORES</u>. Review annual SBTP Forecasts per paragraph 2.a and monthly SBTP Execution reports of participating subordinate squadrons and communicate any changes needed through the chain of command. Ensure any edits to annual forecasts are completed and forecasts submitted/resubmitted by 22 August. Ensure any discrepancies on monthly SBTP Execution reports are reconciled by the 5th working day of the month. MARFOR approval is assumed by COB 22 August for SBTP forecasts and by COB on the 5th working day of the month for SBTP Execution reports unless correspondence is provided to the contrary.

    c. <u>MAWs</u>. Review annual SBTP Forecasts per paragraph 2.a and monthly SBTP Execution reports of participating subordinate squadrons and communicate any changes needed through the chain of command. Ensure any edits to annual forecasts are completed and forecasts submitted/resubmitted by 15 August. Ensure any discrepancies on monthly SBTP Execution reports are reconciled by the 5th working day of the month. MAW approval is assumed by COB 15 August for SBTP forecasts and by COB on the 5th working day of the month for SBTP Execution reports unless correspondence is provided to the contrary. Ensure thorough and accurate information is included in each squadrons' reports.

    d. <u>MCI-East, MCI-West, and Marine Corps Bases Japan</u>. Review annual SBTP Forecasts per paragraph 2.a and monthly SBTP Execution reports of participating subordinate squadrons and communicate any changes needed through the chain of command. Ensure any edits to annual forecasts are completed and forecasts submitted/resubmitted by 15 August. Ensure any discrepancies on monthly SBTP Execution reports are reconciled by the 5th working day of the month. MCI/Marine Corps Bases Japan approval is assumed by COB 15 August for SBTP forecasts and by COB on the 5th working day of the month for SBTP Execution reports unless correspondence is provided to the contrary. Ensure thorough and accurate information is included in the squadrons' reports.

    e. <u>MAGs</u>. Review annual SBTP Forecasts per paragraph 2.a and monthly SBTP Execution reports of participating subordinate squadrons and communicate any changes needed through the chain of command. Ensure any edits to annual forecasts are completed and forecasts submitted/resubmitted by 8 August. Ensure any discrepancies on monthly SBTP Execution reports are reconciled by the 5th working day of the month. MAG approval is assumed by COB 8 August for SBTP forecasts and by COB on the 5th working day of the month for SBTP Execution reports unless correspondence is provided to the contrary. Ensure thorough and accurate information is included in each the squadrons' reports.

f. Squadrons

(1) Annual Unit SBTP Forecast Submission. Develop and submit annual SBTP forecasts per paragraph 2.a by 1 August via M-SHARP. HMM/VMM squadrons should include the hours & sorties of reinforcing units/detachments (HMLA/HMH/VMA) in their SBTP forecast during scheduled MEU/MAGTF operations. Units joining or sending detachments to a composite HMM/VMM squadron should exclude associated hours/sorties from SBTP forecasts during that time. Ensure any edits to annual forecasts directed by senior commands are completed and forecasts resubmitted by the timelines defined above. Squadron approval of SBTP forecasts is indicated by submitting the forecast in M-SHARP.

(2) Monthly Unit SBTP Execution Reporting. Maintain the accuracy of squadron SBTP data in M-SHARP per paragraph 2.b and paragraph 5. Ensure any discrepancies on monthly SBTP Execution reports are reconciled by the 5th working day of the month. Squadron approval is assumed by COB on the 5th working day of the month for SBTP Execution reports unless correspondence is provided to the contrary. Monthly hours & sorties of reinforcing detachments (HMLA/HMH/VMA) assigned to the MEU will be captured via M-SHARP and credited to the HMM/VMM. The automated reporting resident in M-SHARP will eliminate the need for parent commands (HMLA/HMH/VMA) to track flight hours/sorties of detachments assigned to the MEU ACE.

5. Data Accuracy. M-SHARP users shall maintain the integrity of their M-SHARP data for budgeting and accounting purposes. All M-SHARP data used in the SBTP must be maintained at the highest level of accuracy. In order to provide senior commands with information about the accuracy of individual unit data, the health of each unit's M-SHARP program is measured and tracked using the 5 color-coded progression levels below. Each unit's implementation level is objectively assessed by M-SHARP Support Representatives for all levels except Level 1/Green which requires the unit commander's assessment. The current status of all units can be found at https://msharpsupport.com. Squadrons failing to reach Level 1/Green must continue to manually submit the Excel-based "Page 1" and "Page 2" reports via the chain of command.

a. Level 1/Green. Unit is maintaining the requirements for Level 2/Blue, and the Commander has assessed his unit's M-SHARP database accuracy as sufficient for automated reporting to higher headquarters. Commanders or a designated representative shall communicate their Level 1 assessment to TECOM ATB via M-SHARP Support Representatives. Units are required to maintain their M-SHARP program at Level 1/Green.

b. Level 2/Blue. Unit is maintaining the requirements for Level 3/Yellow, has baselined crew data, is logging all flights in M-SHARP, is transferring all flights to NALCOMIS, and is publishing all schedules using M-SHARP (except in cases where schedules are deemed classified) but the Commander has not assessed his unit's M-SHARP database accuracy as sufficient for automated reporting to higher headquarters.

c. Level 3/Yellow. Unit has met the minimum training requirements per NAVMC 35400.14 which is at least one operations representative (officer or enlisted) that has successfully completed the M-SHARP administrators course offered by M-SHARP support representatives. Units are expected to advance to Level 1/Green within three months of receiving training where on-site tech support is available.

d. <u>Level 4/Red</u>. Unit has not met or maintained the minimum training requirements per reference (o). Note that it is possible for a unit to regress from Level 1/Green to Level 4/Red due to turnover of operations personnel. This reflects the strong correlation (verified by more than a decade of supporting data drawn from both the SARA and M-SHARP programs) between adequately-trained personnel and the accuracy of a unit's training management system over time.

e. <u>Level 5/Gray</u>. Unit is not required to use M-SHARP. Level 5/Gray is for units or communities that have not yet been fielded with M-SHARP per the TECOM ATB fielding schedule and for units having received a waiver for M-SHARP usage. Waivers may be requested by message to TECOM ATB via the respective MAW. Units that deployed without M-SHARP are automatically granted a waiver for M-SHARP usage and SBTP deadlines until 60 days after returning from deployment.

6. <u>Technical Support</u>. M-SHARP technical support, training, and troubleshooting assistance are available to users at every level of the chain of command by contacting the M-SHARP Support Team. Contact info is posted on the M-SHARP User Support Site at https://msharpsupport.com/, which also contains the complete M-SHARP Software Users Manual.

Chapter 4

Active Component FHP Fiscal Comptroller Procedures

1. General. The following paragraphs describe the procedures to be used by
the active component FHP Fiscal Comptroller in determining requirements for
the FHP Program.

    a. Funds for the Marine Tactical Aircraft (TACAIR), Fleet Air Training
(FAT), and Fleet Air Support (FAS) FHP are provided by the Operation and
Maintenance, Navy (O&M,N) appropriation, for the sole purpose of supporting
Marine aviation Training and Requirements.

    b. The Marine Forces Commanders provide projected out year flight hour
requirements and possible funding shortfalls during the Program Objective
Memorandum (POM) or Program Review (PR) process. Prior to the beginning of
the Fiscal Year (FY), Type Commanders (TYCOMs) identify projected shortfalls
to OPNAV N4/Financial Management Branch (FMB), providing execution data and
projected cost increases. During the year of execution, MARFORs provide
revised shortfall estimates and request additional funding as part of an
annual mid-year budget review.

2. Activity Group and Sub-Activity Group (AGSAG) are provided the following
funds (according to the following criteria):.

    a. The FHP O&M,N funds are broken into Activity Group (AG) and Sub-
Activity Group (SAG) and allocated to TYCOM LANT/PAC. The MARFOR receive
Operating Target (OPTAR) grants for support of specific T&R operations.

        (1) Activity Group/Sub Activity Group (AGSAG). A four-character
alphanumeric code used in the Operations & Maintenance, Navy (O&M,N);
Operations and Maintenance, Navy Reserve (O&M,NR); Military Personnel, Navy
(MPN); and Reserve Personnel, Navy (RPN) appropriations used to tag resources
by specific purpose. For example, the AGSAG "1C1C" indicates the "Combat
Communications" AGSAG.

        (2) AGSAG 1A1A - 1A - Air Operations. 1A - Mission and other Flight
Operations, which includes Tactical Aircraft (TACAIR) operations and Fleet
Air Support (FAS) operations.

        (3) AGSAG 1A2A - 1A - Air Operations. 2A - Fleet Air Training (FAT)
or Fleet Replacement Squadrons (FRS) train new pilots, refresher or
transition pilots based upon specific Type/Model/Series (T/M/S) aircraft
training syllabi. Aviators returning to flight status from administrative
staffs or non-flying billets attend FRS modified course to refresh/qualify in
their T/M/S.

    b. A complete list of funding and authorized use can be found in NAVSO
P-3013.

3. Operational Functional Category (OFC) can be divided into the following
categories.

    a. Both 1A1A and 1A2A are broken into Operational (or OPTAR) Functional
Category (OFC) to provide specific use of funds (direct or indirect support)
and the type of support the funding provides.

b. The following provides further details of the categories associated with the FHP.

(1) Direct Support. Funds are divided in two OFC, OFC-01 and OFC-50. Each OFC has specifically assigned fund codes which are two digit alphanumeric or numeric-alpha codes that identifies the purpose of the financial transaction and ties the transaction to the appropriate funding.

(a) OFC-01 - Organizational/Squadron Level of Funding. Identified by fund codes 7B for aviation fuels and 7F for flight equipment and administrative supplies in direct support of flight operations and aircraft (A/C) maintenance.

(b) OFC-50 - Intermediate Maintenance Activity (IMA)/Organizational Maintenance Activity (OMA) Level of Funding. Funds support Marine Aircraft Group (MAG), Naval Air Station Aircraft Intermediate Maintenance Department (AIMD), and CV/L-class ships maintenance departments. Identified by fund code 9S for Aviation Depot Level Repairable (AVDLR) repairable components and sub-assemblies, and 7L for aviation fleet maintenance (AFM) non-repairable or consumable parts, bit and piece parts, and contract services.

(2) Indirect Support: Flying Hour Other (FO) funding. Requirements support operations and maintenance of the aircraft and/or essential support of the aviation training, readiness, and maintenance mission.

(a) OFC-09. Individual Material Readiness Lists (IMRL) and Table of Basic Allowance (TBA).

(b) OFC-10. Other Aircraft Services (OAS) to include: Mobile Facilities (MF-vans), Weather (WX), MACS/EAF, Logistics Contractor Support, repair of TBA allowance items.

(c) OFC-21. Temporary Additional Duty (TAD).

(d) OFC-23. Transportation of Things (TOT).

(3) Aviation Training Systems/Simulators (ATS/SIMS). The FHP provides funding to the TYCOMs for ATS/SIMS programs operations. The Navy and Marine Corps simulators are located at multiple training sites in CONUS and OCONUS. NAVAIR Orlando Training Systems Division has the requirement to provide Fielded Training Systems Support (FTSS). TYCOMs budget and provide funds for services to include: Contractor Operation and Maintenance Services (COMS), Contractor Instruction (CI), training device relocations, technical data verification, modifications to training devices and equipment, student management, and other support (e.g., access control, janitorial service, In-Service Engineering Office (ISEO) support, instructional systems development, spare and repair parts provisioning, etc.).

4. Funds Allocation. Funds allocated to the MARFORs are distributed to the MAW for further distribution to the MAG. The MAG Fiscal Officer controls TAD (TACAIR/FRS) funds and, in conjunction with the MALS aviation supply officer, provides Operating Targets (OPTAR) for fuel (7B), flight equipment (7F), aviation maintenance (7L), and AVDLR (9S) to the individual flying squadrons in accordance with reference (i). The MALS Supply Accounting Division (SAD) controls and maintains accounting files and records of the direct and indirect funds (excluding TAD).

5. OFC-01 Budget OPTAR Report (BOR). The OFC-01 Budget OPTAR Report is to be used by all flying squadrons to report: execution of hours and obligations of funds in the following manner. This report is exempt from reports control per reference (m), part IV, paragraph 7.q. The OFC-01 BOR (flying squadrons only) reports execution of the hours and obligations of funds for each T/M/S aircraft assigned. A flying squadron may have multiple OFC-01 BORs, due to multiple Unit Identification Codes (UICs) assigned to a squadron for deployable detachments. The UIC distinguishes the detachment from the main body of the squadron, which allows for individual detachment obligations to be tracked. The BOR submission is mandatory for 18 months, (12 months during the current FY, and 6 months after the closeout of the FY to track financial corrections and/or changes of obligations and expenditure data from the Defense Financial Accounting System (DFAS). A BOR is submitted for an additional 6 months if the Gross Adjusted Obligation (GAO) changes.

a. OFC-01 BOR is the squadron commander's official financial record of obligations and the execution of flight hours for assigned aircraft reported to MAW, MARFOR, and TYCOM. The fuel charges, (identified as 7B fund code), and flight equipment charges (identified as 7F fund code) are summarized on the OFC-01 BOR by T/M/S. OFC-01 7F fund code obligations are funded from OP-20, OFC-50, Aviation Fleet Maintenance (AFM-7L).

b. Weekly transmittals summaries of flight equipment charges (7F) and monthly detailed summary fuel reports of aviation fuel (7B) combine to create a Budget Optar Report (BOR) that provides the TYCOM with account balances and execution information. The TYCOM summarizes all financial accounting records and provides obligations to the Defense Finance and Accounting Service.

c. The squadron commanding officer is responsible for timely and accurate reporting of flying hours for the BOR. The hours listed on the BOR will match the Naval Aviation Flight Record (NAVFLIR) hours recorded in the squadron's NAVFLIR/Naval Aviation Logistics Command Management Information System (NALCOMIS) database. Reconciliation of recorded flight hours between NAVFLIR/NALCOMIS and the BOR will be done daily. The squadron commanding officer must ensure correct and timely information is provided to the MAG in accordance with annual Commander Naval Air Forces (CNAF) guidance.

6. Authorized OFC-01 Charges. OFC-01 funds are for direct support of squadron aircraft operations, fuels (JP/AVGASCOM) fund code 7B, and fund code 7F, consisting of consumable operational supplies (administrative supplies/ServMart: pens, paper, notebooks) and aircrew flight equipment purchases in direct support of flight operations and A/C maintenance.

a. Administrative supplies shall be limited to aircraft maintenance divisions and supporting S-3 operations. Administrative supplies for other than flight related support (i.e., S-1 Personnel) is funded by O&M, MC funds. The squadron commander is responsible for the proper obligation and reporting of funds.

b. There are no discretionary funds within the OFC-01 funding.

c. The following is a list of NAVSO P-3013 authorized OFC-01 charges:

(1) Aviation fuels (JP-4, JP-5, AVGAS, and Commercial fuels) consumed in flight operations.

(2) Pilot/flight crew clothing and operational equipment. Initial and replacement issue of authorized items listed in NAVAIR Allowance List 0035QH series (except items used by maintenance personnel).

(3) Consumable office supplies (aircraft maintenance division and flight operations related S-3 operations only).

(4) Aerial film, recording tape, chart paper used in flight.

(5) Flight deck and safety shoes, used by squadron personnel in the maintenance, launch, and recovery of aircraft.

NOTE: Safety/flight deck shoes used in maintenance shops and with Aviation Maintenance Support Equipment (AMSE) are not chargeable to flight operations, but rather to AFM.

(6) Unit identification marks. Initial issue to newly reported squadron personnel.

(7) Oxygen, liquid and breathing, consumed during flight by both the pilot and aircraft systems.

(8) Shock lubricants and bearing grease. Applicable to flight operations.

(9) Nitrogen. Consumed in flight.

(10) Forms (Cognizance Symbol 1I) and publications. 1I forms, publications, and the reproduction thereof (other than initial outfitting and newly commissioned squadrons or forms and publications used in direct support of maintenance).

(11) Publications that are used to impart technical and professional knowledge (not provided by higher headquarters to officers and enlisted personnel of the command).

(12) Squadron plaques (for commanding and executive officer's offices only).

(13) Special purpose identifying clothing utilized by squadron personnel in the readiness, launch, and recovery of aircraft. Wet suits.

(14) New items published in the aviation safety and survival bulletins for use by pilot or crewmember or other approved Aviation Life Support Systems (ALSS).

(15) Incentive awards, at the discretion of the commanding officer or as approved by TYCOM.

7. Unauthorized OFC-01 Charges

a. Administrative supplies used in support of Morale and Welfare or Marine Corps personnel administrative actions to include personnel records, official correspondence, and command/commanding officer's official support of activities outside of the scope of aviation training and operational readiness requirements.

b. Food or beverages - except for survival rations for aircrew.

c. Commercial services or supplies not related to aviation training and readiness requirements.

d. Computers or peripheral equipment, hardware or software.

e. Gifts or presentations, to include aircraft models/replicas, flight clothing, or other Government procured or issued items.

f. Publications of a recreational nature that contribute to the morale of the command and are not flight operations requirements. Publications that contribute to morale should be provided from the welfare and recreational funds at the discretion of the command.

8. OFC-50 BOR. Monthly summary report of direct maintenance costs for consumables parts and repairable spares are prepared and submitted by the MALS aviation supply officer to the TYCOM, MARFOR, MAW, and MAG. OFC-50 BOR provides the monthly and cumulative obligations for the direct support of aircraft by Type Equipment Code (TEC).

9. Authorized OFC-50 Charges. Direct support of aircraft operations for replacement parts and materials used on aircraft maintenance. The following is a NAVSO P-3013 list of authorized OFC-50 charges.

a. Fund Code 7L -- Consumables

(1) Paints, wiping rags, towel service, cleaning agents and cutting compounds used in preventive maintenance and corrosion control of aircraft and ground support equipment.

(2) Consumable repair parts and miscellaneous material. NSA material used in direct maintenance of aircraft, drones, targets, and component repair or related Ground Support Equipment (GSE).

(3) Pre-expended Bins (PEB), consumable maintenance material meeting requirements for use in maintenance of aircraft, aviation components, GSE, etc.

(4) Aviation Fuels and Lubricants. Aviation fuel and lubricants used in test and check of aircraft engines during engine build up, change or during maintenance (intermediate level only). Petroleum, Oil & Lubricants (POL) products, i.e. oil, fuel additives, or other petroleum products, consumed in flight.

(5) Allowance List Items NAVAIR 00-35-QH. Only items used strictly for maintenance: explosive handlers, face shields, industrial gloves, welders' goggles, and industrial non-prescription safety glasses.

(6) Fuels used in related GSE.

(7) Test bench equipment. Replacement of components used in test bench repair and rotatable pools.

(8) Repairable NSA material having a Material Control code of E, H, G, Q, or X (Non-AVDLR). NSA repairable material (Non-AVDLR) used in maintenance of aircraft.

(9) Maintenance or replacement of aircraft loose equipment listed in the aircraft inventory record.

(10) Hand tools. Consumable hand tools used in the readiness and maintenance of aircraft, maintenance and repair of components and related support equipment.

(11) Safety/Flight Deck Shoes. Used in maintenance shops.

(12) Repair and maintenance of flight clothing and aircrew equipment.

(13) Decals; restricted to decals used on aircraft.

(14) Replacement of Consumable Special Tools and Individual Material Readiness List (IMRL) allowance list items. Cost incurred for IMRL repair.

(15) Packing, Preparation and Preservation. Items consumed in interim packaging/preservation of AFM repairables.

(16) Forms (COG 1I) and Publications. Maintenance Action Form (MAF), bags, equipment condition tags, publications etc., used in support of direct maintenance of aviation components or aircraft.

(17) Special Clothing. Authorized special purpose clothing for dirty work while performing maintenance of aircraft.

(18) Replacements of General Purpose Electronic Test Equipment (GPETE) allowance items, which are missing or unserviceable (COG 7Z).

(19) Civilian field teams (CFT), contract labor support (CLS), or any non-military maintenance contracts charged to direct support of aviation fleet maintenance requires MARFOR approval prior to initiation of contract. Requirements for direct support of aircraft and/or support equipment will be submitted to the MARFOR documenting:

(a) Specific tasking or "statement of work" identifying total requirements.

(b) Longevity of the contract based on calendar dates.

(c) Daily or weekly units of work or production as outlined within the contract agreement.

(d) Recurring weekly, monthly, or annual contracts are not authorized without express approval of MARFOR.

(e) MARFOR will identify and submit all approved CFT/CLS and other maintenance contracts as identified in chapter 6.

(f) MARFOR Assistant Chief of Staff, Aviation Logistics Division (ALD) will conduct annual reviews for requirements and validity of contracts prior to renewal.

b. Fund Code 9S. -- Aviation Depot Level Repairable (AVDLR) or NSA Aviation Depot Level Repairable spare parts.

(1) High cost assemblies repairable at the Intermediate Maintenance Activity (IMA) or MALS maintenance department.

(2) Item has a Standard Unit Price (SUP) and a Net Unit Price (NUP).

(3) SUP is the cost per unit as ordered from the supply system without a corresponding carcass turn-in or exchange.

(4) NUP is a reduced unit price that takes into account the return of repairable carcasses that have been or will be returned to the supply system for repair. The requisition is charged the NUP when the carcass is available for turn-in to the supply system.

(5) In the event the carcass is not returned to the supply system, the SUP is charged. There are designated "grace periods" for CONUS/OCONUS geographical sites to allow for removal, packaging, and return shipment of carcasses to the Naval Supply System Designated Overhaul Point (DOP). However, failure to return the carcass to the supply system within the specified time period results in additional charges to the OFC-50 OPTAR. The additional carcass charges, SUP vice NUP, are significant and impacts directly on the Cost Per Hour (CPH) of the aircraft.

10. Unauthorized OFC-50 Charges

a. Any charges of materials, parts, or supplies not directly related to the maintenance or support of aircraft, aviation ground support equipment, or aviation peculiar support equipment.

b. Buildings and grounds upkeep.

c. Additional items such as:

(1) Shipment of aviation parts Ready for Issue (RFI) or Non-RFI, materials, or any organic supplies and equipment. Transportation charges for Government or commercial shipments or shipping services to include Fedex, UPS, and other CONUS/OCONUS shipments.

(2) Office equipment leases or purchases, to include copiers, computers, and other labor saving administrative equipment.

(3) Non-aviation related services or support agreements.

(4) Facilities, building and grounds, and runway/ramp repairs or renovation.

(5) Furniture, household-cleaning supplies, material handling equipment or services.

(6) Transportation or vehicle rental agreements other than aircraft handling/towing equipment. (See Transportation of Things charges.)

(7) Mailing or correspondence materials and services.

(8) Civilian labor, software, or technical services requirements not approved by the TYCOM.

(9) Food and beverages.

11. CPH. The CPH for a specific aircraft is computed by adding all related direct support requirements from the OFC-01 BOR, and the OFC-50 BOR total obligations, and fair share of miscellaneous charges. Fair share is a percentage of miscellaneous charges based on the number of aircraft divided by the number of executed hours over the same time period. The monthly CPH for each T/M/S must be derived from three sources and combined for the Total CPH:

a. The OFC-01 BOR charges are calculated as follows:

(1) OFC-01 Fuel (7B) obligations for each T/M/S divided by executed hours = Fuel CPH.

Example: F/A-18C ($8,805,126 ÷ 8,304.3 HOURS) = $1,060 Fuel CPH

(2) OFC-01 Flt Equipment (7F) obligations for each T/M/S divided by executed hours = Flight Equipment CPH.

Example: F/A-18C ($830,430 ÷ 8,304.3 HOURS) = $100

b. The OFC-50 BOR for obligations at the MAG/IMA level of maintenance support. The CPH for AFM (7L) and AVDLR (9S) equation is as follows:

Obligations by T/M/S divided by hours for all squadrons = CPH (less TYCOM withholds).

(1) Example: Obligations for F/A-18C ÷ Hours for F/A-18C = CPH

OR

(2) AFM (7L)   (14,050,589 ÷ 8,304.3) = $1,691 CPH
    AVDLR (9S)   (22,027,553 ÷ 8,304.3) = $2,652 CPH

c. TYCOM withholds, funding documents, fund codes 7B, 7F, 7L, and 9S, for services, parts, and contracts in support of specific T/M/S generated by squadron/MAG requirements for external support of the squadron/aircraft are added to the I-Level CPH by the TYCOM. Therefore, it is essential that all charges be tracked for accuracy and validity against each T/M/S of aircraft.

12. Indirect Support. Commonly referred to as Flying Hour Other (FO) accounts require the same reporting as direct support OFCs. FO costs are not considered in the CPH calculations. However, the impact of under-funding FO accounts impacts significantly on the overall FHP.

a. Authorized IMRL/TBA OFC-09 Charges:

(1) Individual Material Readiness Lists (IMRL) OFC-09 - NSA Material Individual Material Readiness List (IMRL) initial issue.

(2) Marine Table of Basic Allowance (TBA), OFC-09 - Approved and authorized allowance items initial issue.

b. Unauthorized IMRL/TBA OFC-09 Charges:

(1) Purchase/requisition of non-IMRL/TBA allowance list items.

(2) Services or repairs of IMRL/TBA items.

(3) Contract and contract support.

c. Authorized Other Aircraft Services (OAS) OFC-10 Charges:

(1) Mobile Maintenance Facilities (MMF-vans) - repairs, preventative maintenance and replacements of parts for the vans, air conditioning, and generator support.

(2) External Training Loads, Targets, Tow Banners, and Dunnage.

(3) Weather (WX) - Authorized maintenance and repair parts, supplies, and services related to aviation support.

(4) MACS - Authorized maintenance and repair parts, supplies, and services related to aviation support.

(5) Logistics/Technical Contractor Support - Authorized technical assistance and training support contractors approved by MARFOR. Contractors for technical, logistics or maintenance support charged to indirect support requires MARFOR approval prior to initiation of the contract. Requirements will be submitted to the MARFOR documenting:

(a) Specific tasking or "statement of work" identifying total requirements.

(b) Longevity of the contract based on calendar dates.

(c) Daily or weekly units of work or production as outlined within the contract agreement.

(d) Recurring weekly, monthly, or annual contracts are not authorized without express approval of MARFOR.

(e) MARFOR will identify and submit all approved maintenance contracts as identified in chapter 6.

(f) MARFOR Assistant Chief of Staff, Aviation Logistics Division (ALD) will conduct annual reviews for requirements and validity of contracts prior to renewal.

(6) Repair of TBA allowance end items - Authorized maintenance and repair parts, supplies, and services related to aviation support.

(7) Range fees and airfield operations charges in support of aviation training and readiness missions.

d. Unauthorized OAS OFC-10 Charges. Obligations that are not specifically for the support of the aircraft readiness or maintenance requirements as listed above. Transportation or shipping services for any purpose.

e. Authorized TAD OFC-21 Charges

(1) Temporary Additional Duty (TAD) travel and per diem charges for aviation support or related requirements for military and Government employees (GS).

(2) School quotas for aviation squadron or unit training.

(3) Squadron or unit training for aviation related readiness.

(4) Factory maintenance training.

(5) TRANS-PACIFIC or TRANS-ATLANTIC for aircrew and maintenance support personnel regardless of the change of custody of the aircraft.

(6) Crew rotation (CONUS)-Rotation of crews within squadron.

(7) Travel and per diem for military and Government employees to conduct site visits and inspections of aviation logistics and maintenance operations ashore or afloat.

(8) Site surveys for air operations and deployments. Attendance at aviation related planning or technical conferences.

(9) Deployment (within/outside CONUS).

(10) Emergency quarters while on extended flight.

f. Unauthorized TAD OFC-21 Charges

(1) Funding of travel for military spouses and/or family members, civilian contractors, or non-Government employees are not authorized.

(2) Funding military personnel or Government employees traveling for non-aviation related support to include conferences, seminars, and site visits.

(3) Funding travel of emergency leave or morale leave.

(4) Funding travel for personal business or official business not related to the support of aircraft or Marine Aviation.

g. Authorized Transportation of Things (TOT) OFC-23 Charges

(1) TOT, OFC-23, includes costs of transportation of ready for issue (RFI) aviation parts, materials, and related things chargeable to aviation operating force funds. Trans-shipment of supply system parts via Government shipping channels to include Air Mobility Command (AMC), Military Sealift Command (MSC), or contract commercial sources (Fedex/UPS/DHL) as appropriate to meet delivery date requirements.

(2) Costs are limited to transportation of organic (squadron owned) aviation material to include support equipment and maintenance tools in support of aviation operations and training.

(3) The TYCOM establishes and funds Transportation Account Codes (TAC) for transportation and movement of TOT in support of specific operations and exercises. The TAC permits units to cite the appropriate TAC for billing of AMC, MSC, or commercial carriers obligations. MARFOR TOT funds are withheld by the TYCOM to cover individual unit TAC obligations.

(4) Packaging and preservation materials and supplies used in processing authorized shipments of aviation parts and support equipment.

(5) Lease/rental agreements for forklifts, flight line delivery vehicles and other materials handling equipment.

(6) Transportation or vehicle lease/rental agreements other than aircraft handling/towing equipment used to support flight line operations, delivery and movement of aircraft parts and supplies.

h. Unauthorized TOT OFC-23 Charges

(1) Shipment of Non-RFI components to depot level or commercial repair sites (CONUS or OCONUS) or to other Naval Supply System designated activities.

(2) Transportation, packaging, or storage of personal effects, household goods, or privately owned vehicles. These charges should be referred to the appropriate Transportation Management Office (TMO) for proper entitlements and/or disposition.

(3) Commercial shipping agreement contracts or services (Fedex, UPS, or other commercial shippers) not specifically approved by MARFORs ALD and the TYCOM.

13. <u>Contingency Operations</u>. The policies and procedures for the funding of contingency operations are provided in the following paragraphs.

a. A military operation that is either designated by the Secretary of Defense as a contingency operation or becomes a contingency operation as a matter of law. Contingency operations hours are conducted in support of contingency operations as delineated by the TYCOM directions. The following definitions apply.

(1) Contingency flight hours: hours flown on any flight in direct support of a contingency operation. All flights that originate in country, regardless of mission, are considered contingency flights. Flights that originate outside the contingency operation area (i.e. from sea or an allied country) only count as contingency flights if they are in direct support of the operation. Contingency flight hours are reported monthly by the squadron in the Budget OPTAR report.

(2) Incremental contingency flight hours: contingency flight hours flown above the baseline flight hour allotment. All contingency hours flown by activated reserve squadrons are incremental contingency hours. All contingency hours flown by AC squadrons that are above the training hours planned in the squadron's SBTP are incremental contingency hours. Incremental contingency hours are reported monthly by the MARFOR in the Flying Hour Cost Report.

b. The MARFORs are responsible for the accurate and timely reporting of contingency hours and financial obligations. Assistant Chief of Staff, G-3/ Comptroller/G-8 will document, record, report, and maintain files for contingency hours and obligated funding for contingency operation(s). Execution data of contingency hours will reflect total hours and total costs for each contingency operation and will be maintained as separate entities from baseline hours and cost. The execution data will be maintained by contingency location (for multiple sites and/or deployments), aircraft T/M/S, and funding category obligations (fuel/consumables/contracts/AVDLR/FO). FHP CPH costs and Flying Hours Other (FO) costs will reflect ongoing operations, identifying organic and activated reserve squadrons' costs as separate entities for financial reporting purposes.

(1) MARFORs will ensure costs for each T/M/S are inclusive of active duty and activated reserve squadrons funded directly or indirectly by funding documents or reimbursable funds.

(2) Organic squadron contingency hours will be identified and reflected in total hours and costs by the reporting squadron as directed by MARFOR/TYCOM via the BOR(s) monthly for direct and indirect support.

(3) Contingency hours, for organic squadrons and activated reserve squadrons, will be reconciled monthly between the active MAW, 4th MAW, and the MARFOR (G-3 for executed hours and Comptroller/G-8 for obligated costs).

(4) The MARFOR Comptroller/G-8 will reconcile with the TYCOM for contingency hours and supporting financial obligation reports. Reports will maintain continuity and accuracy for financial obligations.

c. Supplemental Funds. Incremental contingency hours and indirect costs associated with contingency operations are funded by supplemental funds to relieve the TYCOM of having to fund costs in excess of OP-20 budgeted hours. Supplemental funds are requested by the TYCOM based on an "approved" contingency operation. TYCOMs must request supplemental from FMB.

d. Over-executed flight hours not flown in support of a contingency operation(s) will not be funded. Additionally, if the sum of training hours and those executed in support of contingencies does not exceed SBTP programmed hours it is not considered for supplemental funds. These costs are the internal responsibility of the MARFORs or TYCOM.

e. T&R flight hours lost (under-executed or not executed) while supporting contingency operations shall not be flown in addition to programmed T&R hours for subsequent months of execution or flown in excess scheduled hours in other squadron(s) with same/similar aircraft or missions, unless mission requirements dictate.

f. Movement of under-executed flight hours to satisfy T&R requirements for a squadron's lost hours should be done to create normal utilization of aircraft and to complete aircrew T&R requirements. Over-flying to meet total execution of MAW SBTP is prohibited. Each hour should reflect a T&R requirement and a corresponding contingency hours offsets.

14. Activated Reserve Unit Flight Hour Funding Procedures

a. Upon activation (as defined in chapter 6 and Joint Publication 1-02), all the RC unit flight hour costs will be funded entirely via O&M,N by the gaining AC MARFOR, regardless of where the activated RC unit is operating. Upon deactivation, the RC unit's FHP funding will revert back to O&M,NR funding through MARFORRES. It is incumbent upon the activated RC unit to report their unexecuted flight hour funds to 4th MAW for submission to MARFORRES.

b. MARFORRES/4th MAW will report all activated unit's remaining unexecuted Flight Hour funds to Commander Naval Reserve Forces Command for submission to OPNAV N-82 Financial Management Branch (FMB) for reprogramming. FMB will submit the reprogramming initiative to OSD with CMC advocacy. The intent is to source the gaining AC MARFOR budget shortfall with the unexecuted reserve flight hour funds.

c. Activated reserve squadron hours for both contingency operations and CONUS training will be logged by aircrew, identified by T/M/S, and reported monthly to the TYCOM using their activated ORG code (listed below) as coordinated by the MARFOR and MARFORRES/4th MAW. The MARFOR providing the financial resources for the activated reserve squadron(s) will report the executed hours and costs.

Reserve Unit Activated Organizational Codes

Reserve Component Unit	ORG Code	Activated ORG Code
HMM-764	SL3	SM4
HMM-774	SN1	SN3
HMLA-773	SE4	SQ1
HMH-772	SU5	SU9
VMFA-112	SD2	SD7
VMFA-134	SL1	SM4
VMFA-142	SJ1	SJ3
VMGR-234	SA3	SA6, SA7
VMGR-452	SM1	SM2

15. Frequently Used Financial Acronyms. The table of frequently used acronyms in the FHP Program is listed below in order to enable commanders to have an easily accessible source of information.

AFM	Aviation Fleet Maintenance
AG	Activity Group
AIMD	Aviation Intermediate Maintenance Department
ASD	Aviation Supply Department
ASHE	Aviation Support Handling Equipment
AVDLR	Aviation Depot Level Repairable
BISOG	Blue (Navy $$) in Support of Green (USMC $$)
BOR	Budget Operating Report
CLS	Contractor Logistics Support
CNAF	Commander, Naval Air Forces (see CNAP)
CNAL	Commander, Naval Air Forces, Atlantic
CNAP	Commander, Naval Air Forces, Pacific
DFAS	Defense Financial and Accounting Services
FAS	Fleet Air Support
FAT	Fleet Air Training (see FRS)
FHP	Flying Hour Program
FHPS	Flying Hour Projection System
FRS	Fleet Replacement Squadron (see FAT)
GSE	Ground Support Equipment
IMA	Intermediate Maintenance Activity
IMRL	Individual Material Requirements List
MACP	Marine Aviation Campaign Plan
MALS	Marine Aviation Logistics Squadron
MARFOR(COM/PAC/RES)	Commander, U.S. Marine Forces (Command/Pacific/RESERVE)
MF vans	Mobile Facilities vans
MFC/MFP	MARFORCOM/MARFORPAC
OAS	Other Aircraft Services
OFC	Operational Functional Category
OMN	Operational and Maintenance, Navy
OP-20	Flying Hour Program DON Budget Exhibit
PMAA	Primary Mission Aircraft Authorization
POM	Program Objective Memorandum (even year)
PPBE	Planning, Programming, Budgeting, Execution
PR	Program Review (odd year)
SAD	Aviation Supply Accounting Division

SAG	Sub Activity Group
TACAIR	Tactical Aircraft
TAD	Temporary Additional Duty
TBA	Table of Basic Allowance
TECOM	Training and Education Command
TL	Transmittal
TMS	Type Model Series of Aircraft
TOT	Transportation of Things
TYCOM	Type Commander

Chapter 5

Reserve Component FHP Fiscal Comptroller Procedures

1. General

   a. Funds for the Marine Aviation Reserve Flying Hour Program (FHP) are provided by the Operations and Maintenance, Navy Reserve (O&M,NR) appropriation, for the sole purpose of supporting Reserve Marine Aviation Training and Readiness requirements.

   b. 4th MAW G-3 provides out year estimated flight hours and identifies budget shortfalls during the Program Objective Memorandum (POM) or Program Review (PR) process. Commander Naval Reserve Forces Command (CNRFC) N-8 addresses shortfalls to OPNAV N4/FMB as required providing execution data and projected cost increases. In the year of execution, during the CNRFC N-8's mid-year budget review process, 4th MAW provides revised shortfall estimates and requests additional funding as required.

2. Activity Group and Sub-Activity Group (AGSAG)

   a. The FHP, O&M,NR funds are broken into activity group (AG) and sub-activity Group (SAG), and allocated to the CNRFC N-8. Site comptrollers receive operating target (OPTAR) grants, with the guidance from 4th MAW Aviation Logistics Division, for support of specific training and readiness (T&R) operations.

   b. AGSAG is a four-character alphanumeric code used in the O&M,NR appropriation used to tag resources by specific purpose. For example, the AGSAG "1A1A" indicates the "Flight Hour Funding" AGSAG.

   c. A complete list of funding and authorized use can be found in reference (a).

3. Reserve Funding Categories

   a. The Reserve funding categories contain both direct funding and indirect funding. The following provides more detail on the funding categories associated with the Reserve FHP:

      (1) Direct Support. Funds are divided in four flight-funding categories: fuel, organizational maintenance activity (OMA), intermediate maintenance activity (IMA) and Aviation Depot Level Repairables (AVDLR).

         (a) Fuel. Organizational/Squadron level of funding. This category of funding is for fuel, flight equipment and administrative supplies (Serv-Mart).

         (b) OMA, IMA, and AVDLR funding. Funds support Reserve Marine squadrons, Reserve Naval Air Station Aircraft Intermediate Maintenance Department (AIMD) as well as Aviation Depot Level Repairable (AVDLR) repairable components and sub-assemblies, Aviation Fleet Maintenance OMA/IMA non-repairable or consumable parts, bit and piece parts, and contract services.

      (2) Indirect Support. Flying hour other (FO) funding supports operations and maintenance of the aircraft and/or essential support of aviation training, readiness, and maintenance mission. Categories are:

(a) Individual Material Readiness Lists (IMRL) and Table of Basic Allowance (TBA).

(b) Other Aircraft Services (OAS), to include mobile facilities (MF-vans), Weather (WX), Marine Corps Air Station (MCAS)/Expeditionary Air Field (EAF), logistics contractor support, repair of TBA allowance items.

(c) Temporary Additional Duty (TAD).

(d) Transportation of Things (TOT).

(3) Aviation Training Systems/Simulators (ATS/SIMS). The FHP provides funding to the CNRFC N-8 for ATS/SIMS programs operations. The Navy and Marine Corps Reserves simulators are located at multiple training sites in CONUS. NAVAIR Orlando Training Systems Division has the requirement to provide Fielded Training Systems Support (FTSS) Services. CNRFC N-8 budgets and provide funds for services to include: contractor operation and maintenance services (COMS), contractor instruction (CI), training device relocations, technical data verification, modifications to training devices and equipment, student management, and other support (e.g., access control, janitorial service, In-Service Engineering Office (ISEO) support, instructional systems development, spare and repair parts provisioning, etc).

4. Funds Allocation. Funds allocated to the Marine Reserves are distributed to the site comptrollers for further distribution to the Marine Reserve Squadrons. The site comptrollers provide OPTAR for fuel, OMA, IMA and AVDLR to the individual flying squadrons. Funding received from the site comptroller is entered into Fund Administration and Standardized Data Automation (FAST DATA), which produce the OPTARs for each category. These OPTARs are established to ensure funding is available before a requirement is released into the system. The aviation supply officer controls TAD funds for the squadron(s) at that site.

5. Flight Hour Cost Report (FHCR). The FHCR (flying squadrons only) reports execution of the hours and cumulative obligations for the direct support of aircraft by Type Equipment Code (TEC). Individual detachment(s) obligations will be tracked and reported separately on the FHCR. Site comptrollers are required to submit the monthly FHCR to CNRFC N-8 within the first 10 working days of the month (by the 15th). This report is exempt from reports control per reference (m), part IV, paragraph 7.q.

a. The FHCR is the squadron commander's official financial record of obligations and the execution of flight hours for assigned aircraft reported to 4th MAW and CNRFC N-8. The fuel charges and flight equipment charges are summarized on the FHCR by T/M/S.

b. The squadron's commanding officer (S-3) is responsible for timely and accurate reporting of flying hours for the FHCR. The hours listed on the FHCR will match the Naval Aviation Flight Record (NAVFLIR) hours recorded in the squadron's NAVFLIR/Naval Aviation Logistics Management Information System (NALCOMIS) database. Reconciliation of recorded flight hours between NAVFLIR/NALCOMIS and the FHCR will be conducted on a daily basis. Corrective action shall be taken prior to monthly submission of the FHCR and NAVFLIR reports.

6. Authorized Fuel Charges. Fuel funds are for direct support of squadron aircraft operations, fuels jet petroleum (JP)/aviation gas commercial (AVGASCOM), consumable operational supplies (administrative supplies/ServMart - pens, paper, notebooks) and pilots and aircrew flight equipment purchases.

a. Administrative supplies shall be limited to aircraft maintenance divisions and supporting flight operations. Administrative supplies for other than flight related support (i.e., S-1 Personnel) are funded by O&M,MCR funds. The squadron commander is responsible for the proper obligation and reporting of funds.

b. There are no discretionary funds within the fuel funding category.

c. The following is a list of NAVSO P-3013 authorized fuel charges:

(1) Aviation fuels (JP-4, JP-5, AVGAS, and commercial fuels), consumed in flight operations.

(2) Aircrew clothing and operational equipment. Includes initial and replacement issue of authorized items listed in NAVAIR Allowance List 0035QH series (except items used by maintenance personnel).

(3) Consumable office supplies (aircraft maintenance division and related S-3 operations only).

(4) Aerial film, recording tape, chart paper used in flight.

(5) Flight deck and safety shoes used by squadron personnel in the maintenance, and launch and recovery of aircraft. Safety/flight deck shoes used in maintenance shops and with Aviation Maintenance Support Equipment (AMSE) are not chargeable to flight operations, but rather to aviation fleet maintenance.

(6) Unit Identification Marks. Initial issue to newly reported squadron personnel.

(7) Oxygen, liquid and breathing, consumed during flight by both the pilot and aircraft systems.

(8) Shock lubricants and bearing grease. Applicable to flight operations.

(9) Nitrogen consumed in flight.

(10) Forms, publications, and the reproduction thereof (other than initial outfitting of newly commissioned squadrons, or forms and publications used in direct support of maintenance).

(11) Publications used to impart technical and professional knowledge (not provided by higher headquarters to officers and enlisted personnel of the command).

(12) Squadron plaques for units only; not for personal awards, except for commanding and executive officers' offices.

(13) Special purpose identifying clothing utilized by squadron personnel in the maintenance, launch, and recovery of aircraft and wet suits.

(14) New items published in the aviation safety and survival bulletins for use by pilot or crewmember or approved Aviation Life Support Systems (ALSS).

(15) Incentive awards at the discretion of the commanding officer, or as approved by TYCOM.

7. Unauthorized Charges

a. Administrative supplies used in support of morale and welfare or Marine Corps personnel administrative actions to include personnel records, official correspondence, and command/commanding officer's official support of activities outside of the scope of aviation training and operational readiness requirements.

b. Food or beverages; except for survival rations for pilot/aircrew.

c. Commercial services or supplies not related to aviation T&R requirements.

d. Computers, peripheral equipment, and software.

e. Gifts or presentations, to include aircraft models/replicas, flight clothing, or other Government procured or issued items.

f. Publications of a recreational nature that contribute to the morale of the command that are not flight operations requirements. Publications that contribute to morale should be provided from the welfare and recreational funds at the discretion of the command.

8. Authorized OMA, IMA and AVDLR Charges. Direct support of aircraft operations for replacement parts and materials used on aircraft maintenance. The following is a list of authorized charges in accordance with reference (a):

a. OMA and IMA Consumables

(1) Paints, wiping rags, towel service, cleaning agents, and cutting compounds used in preventive maintenance and corrosion control of aircraft and ground support equipment.

(2) Consumable repair parts and miscellaneous material. Naval Support Activity (NSA) material used in direct maintenance of aircraft, drones, targets, and component repair or related Ground Support Equipment (GSE).

(3) Pre-expended Bins (PEB), consumable maintenance material meeting requirements of use in maintenance of aircraft, aviation components, GSE, etc.

(4) Aviation fuel and lubricants used in the testing of aircraft engines during engine build up, change or during maintenance (intermediate level only). Petroleum, Oil & Lubricants (POL) products, i.e., oil, fuel additives, or other petroleum products, consumed in flight.

(5) Allowance list items; only items used strictly for maintenance: explosive handlers, face shields, industrial gloves, welders' goggles, and industrial non-prescription safety glasses.

(6) Fuels used in related GSE.

(7) Test Bench Equipment. Replacement of components used in test bench repair and rotatable pools.

(8) Repairable NSA material having a material control code of E, H, G, Q, or X (Non-AVDLR). NSA repairable material (Non-AVDLR) used in maintenance of aircraft.

(9) Maintenance or replacement of aircraft loose equipment listed in the aircraft inventory record.

(10) Consumable hand tools used in the readiness and maintenance of aircraft, maintenance and repair of components and related support equipment.

(11) Safety/flight deck shoes used in maintenance shops.

(12) Repair and maintenance of flight clothing and pilots/crew equipment.

(13) Decals; restricted to decals used on aircraft.

(14) Replacement of consumable special tools and IMRL allowance list items, and cost incurred for IMRL repair.

(15) Packing, Preparation and Preservation. Items consumed in interim packaging/preservation of aviation fleet maintenance repairables.

(16) Forms and Publications. Maintenance Action Form (MAF), MAF Bags, equipment condition tags, publications, etc., used in support of direct maintenance of aviation components or aircraft.

(17) Authorized special purpose clothing for dirty work while performing maintenance of aircraft.

(18) Replacements of General Purpose Electronic Test Equipment (GPETE) allowance items, which are missing or unserviceable (COG 7Z).

(19) Civilian field teams (CFT); contract labor support (CLS), or any non-military maintenance contracts charged to direct support of aviation fleet maintenance requires MARFOR/4th MAW approval prior to initiation of contract. Requirements for direct support of aircraft and/or support equipment will be submitted to the MARFOR/4th MAW documenting:

(a) Specific tasking or "statement of work" identifying total requirements.

(b) Longevity of the contract based on calendar dates.

(c) Daily or weekly units of work or production as outlined within the contract agreement.

(d) Recurring weekly, monthly, or annual contracts are not authorized without express approval of 4th MAW and CNRFC N-8.

(e) 4th MAW Assistant Chief of Staff, Aviation Logistics Division (ALD) will conduct annual reviews for requirements and validity of contracts prior to renewal.

b. AVDLR or NSA ADLR

(1) High cost assemblies repairable at the IMA or MALS maintenance department.

(2) Items have a standard unit price (SUP) and a net unit price (NUP).

(a) SUP is the cost per unit as ordered from the supply system without a corresponding carcass turn-in or exchange.

(b) NUP is a reduced unit price for carcass charges that have been or will be returned to the supply system for repair. The requisition is charged the NUP when the carcass is available for turn-in to the supply system.

(c) In the event the carcass is not returned to the supply system, the SUP is charged. There are designated "grace periods" for CONUS/OCONUS geographical sites to allow for removal, packaging, and return shipment of carcasses to the Naval Supply System Designated Overhaul Point (DOP). However, failure to return the carcass to the supply system within the specified time period results in additional charges to the AVDLR OPTAR. The additional carcass charges, standard price vice net price, are significant and impacts directly on the CPH of the aircraft.

9. Unauthorized OMA, IMA and AVDLR Charges

a. Any charges of materials, parts, or supplies not directly related to the maintenance or support of aircraft, aviation ground support equipment, or aviation-peculiar support equipment.

b. Buildings and grounds upkeep.

c. Additional items such as:

(1) Shipment of aviation parts (RFI or Non-RFI), materials, or any organic supplies and equipment. Transportation charges for government or commercial shipments or shipping services to include FEDEX, UPS, and other CONUS/OCONUS shipments.

(2) Office equipment leases or purchases, to include copiers, computers, and other labor-saving administrative equipment.

(3) Non-aviation related services or support agreements.

(4) Facilities, building and grounds, and runway/ramp repairs or renovation.

(5) Furniture, household-cleaning supplies, material handling equipment or services.

(6) Transportation or vehicle rental agreements other than aircraft handling/towing equipment.

(7) Mailing or correspondence materials and services.

(8) Civilian labor, software, or technical services requirements not approved by the TYCOM.

(9) Food and beverages.

10. Cost Per Hour (CPH). The CPH for a specific aircraft is computed by adding all related direct support requirements from the FHCR (fuel, OMA, IMA

and AVDLR) to the total obligations, and dividing by the number of executed hours within the same time period.

a. Fuel obligations for each Type/Model/Series (T/M/S) divided by executed hours = Fuel CPH.

Example: F/A-18A ($8,805,126 ÷ 8,304.3 Hours) = $1,060 Fuel CPH

b. Obligations by T/M/S divided by hours for all squadrons = CPH (less CNRFC N-8 withholds). The CPH for OMA, IMA and AVDLR equation is as follows:

(1) Example: Obligations for F/A-18A ÷ Hours for F/A-18A = CPH

OR

(2) OMA/IMA   (14,050,589 ÷ 8,304.3) = $1,691 CPH
    AVDLR   (22,027,553 ÷ 8,304.3) = $2,652 CPH

11. <u>Indirect Support</u>. Commonly referred to as Flying Hour Other (FO) accounts require the same reporting as direct support. FO costs are not considered in the CPH calculations. However, under-funding FO accounts impacts significantly on the overall FHP.

a. <u>Authorized IMRL/TBA Charges</u>

(1) Individual Material Readiness Lists (IMRL); NSA Material and (IMRL) initial issue.

(2) Marine Table of Basic Allowance (TBA); approved allowance items initial issue and replacement.

b. <u>Unauthorized IMRL/TBA Charges</u>

(1) Purchase/requisition of non-IMRL/TBA allowance list items.

(2) Services or repairs of IMRL/TBA items.

(3) Contract or contractor support.

c. <u>Authorized OAS Charges</u>

(1) Mobile facilities (MF-vans); repairs, preventative maintenance and replacements of parts for the vans, air conditioning, and generator support.

(2) Weather (WX); authorized maintenance and repair parts, supplies, and services related to aviation support.

(3) MACS/EAF; authorized maintenance and repair parts, supplies, and services related to aviation support.

(4) Logistics/Technical Contractor Support; authorized technical assistance and training support contractors approved by CNRFC/N-8/4th MAW. Contractors for technical, logistics, or maintenance support charged to indirect support requires CNRFC/N-8/4th MAW approval prior to initiation of the contract. Requirements will be submitted to the CNRFC/N-8/4th MAW documenting:

(a) specific Specific tasking or "statement of work" identifying total requirements.;

(b) longevity Longevity of the contract based on calendar dates.;

(c) daily Daily or weekly units of work or production as outlined within the contract agreement.;

(d) recurring Recurring weekly, monthly, or annual contracts are not authorized without express approval of CNRFC/N-8/4th MAW.;

(e) 4th MAW/CNRFC N-8 will identify and submit all approved maintenance contracts as identified in enclosure 7. "Contract Maintenance Report". and

(f) 4th MAW Assistant Chief of Staff, ALD and CNRFC N-8 will conduct annual reviews for requirements and validity of contracts prior to renewal.

(5) Repair of TBA allowance end items - authorized maintenance and repair parts, supplies, and services related to aviation support.

(6) Range fees and airfield operations charges in support of aviation T&R missions. These charges are handled directly by CNRFC N-8.

d. <u>Unauthorized OAS Charges</u>. Obligations that are not specifically for the support of the aircraft maintenance requirements as listed above, as well as transportation or shipping services for any purpose.

e. <u>Authorized TAD Charges</u>

(1) Temporary Additional Duty (TAD) travel and per diem charges for aviation support or related requirements for military and Government employees.

(2) School quotas for aviation squadron or unit training.

(3) Squadron or unit training for aviation related readiness.

(4) Factory maintenance training.

(5) Trans-Pacific or Trans-Atlantic for aircrew and maintenance support personnel regardless of the chain of custody of the aircraft.

(6) Crew Rotation (CONUS). Rotation of crews within squadron.

(7) Travel and per diem for military and Government employees to conduct site visits and inspections of aviation logistics and maintenance operations ashore or afloat.

(8) Site surveys for air operations and deployments. Attendance at aviation related planning or technical conferences.

(9) Deployment (within/outside CONUS).

(10) Emergency quarters while on extended missions.

f. Unauthorized TAD Charges

(1) Funding of travel for military spouses and/or family members, civilian contractors, or non-government employee is not authorized.

(2) Funding military personnel or Government employees traveling for non-aviation related support to include conferences, seminars, and site visits.

(3) Funding travel of emergency leave or morale leave.

(4) Funding travel for personal business or official business not related to the support of aircraft or Marine Aviation.

g. Authorized TOT Charges

(1) Transportation of Things (TOT) includes costs of transportation of ready for issue (RFI) aviation parts, materials, and related things chargeable to aviation operating force funds. Trans-shipment of supply system parts via Government shipping channels to include Air Mobility Command (AMC), Military Sealift Command (MSC), or contract commercial sources (FEDEX/UPS/DHL) as appropriate to meet delivery date requirements.

(2) Costs are limited to transportation of organic (squadron owned) aviation material to include support equipment and maintenance tools in support aviation operations and training.

(3) The CNRFC N-8 and 4th MAW ALD-C establishes and funds Transportation Account Codes (TAC) for transportation and movement of TOT in support of specific operations and exercises. The TAC permits units to cite the appropriate TAC for billing of AMC, MSC, or commercial carriers obligations. TOT funds are withheld by the 4th MAW/site comptrollers to cover individual unit TAC obligations.

(4) Packaging and preservation materials and supplies used in processing authorized shipments of aviation parts and support equipments.

(5) Lease/rental agreements for forklifts, flight line delivery vehicles and other materials handling equipment.

(6) Transportation or vehicle lease/rental agreements other than aircraft handling/towing equipment used to support flight line operations, delivery and movement of aircraft parts and supplies.

h. Unauthorized TOT Charges

(1) Shipment of Non-RFI components to depot level or commercial repair sites (CONUS or OCONUS) or to other Naval Supply System designated activities.

(2) Transportation, packaging, or storage of personal effects, household goods or privately owned vehicles. These charges should be referred to the appropriate Transportation and Movement Office (TMO) for proper disposition.

(3) Commercial shipping agreement contracts or services (Fedex, UPS, or other commercial shippers) not specifically approved by 4th MAW ALD and the CNRFC N-8.

12. Reserve Activation and Contingency Operations

a. Upon activation, the Gaining Force Command (GFC) will fund, via O&M,N, all flight hour operations to include Flying Hour Other(FO) costs. Activated reserve squadrons are funded, directly or indirectly, by reimbursable funds for all contingency flight hours.

(1) Direct Funding. The activated reserve squadron is attached to an active duty MAW that supplies all support required. On the activation date, the activated reserve squadron is funded by the GFC through the MAW.

(2) Indirect Funding. The activated reserve squadron, when not directly attached to an active duty MAW, is funded on the activation date by reimbursable documents from the GFC sent to Navy Reserve site comptrollers.

b. Contingency Operations. A military operation that is either designated by the Secretary of Defense as a contingency operation, or becomes a contingency operation as a matter of law. Contingency operations flight hours are conducted in support of contingency operations as delineated by the TYCOM directions. For budgeting purposes, contingency hours are "executed hours," flown as direct or indirect support of designated contingency operation(s).

c. MARFORCOM/MARFORPAC/4th MAW is responsible for the accurate and timely reporting of contingency hours and financial obligations. Assistant Chief of Staff, G-3/4th MAW ALD-C will document, record, report, and maintain files for contingency hours and obligated funding for contingency operations. Execution data of contingency hours will reflect total hours and total costs for each contingency operation and be maintained as separate entities by contingency location (for multiple sites and/or deployments), aircraft T/M/S, and funding category obligations (fuel/consumables/ contracts/AVDLR/FO). CPH and (FO) costs will reflect ongoing operations, identifying activated reserve squadrons costs as separate entities for financial reporting purposes.

(1) Activated reserve squadron contingency hours, when using direct funding, will be identified by T/M/S and reported monthly to the TYCOM as coordinated by the MARFOR. The MARFOR providing the financial resources for the activated reserve squadron(s) will report the executed hours and costs. This report is exempt from reports control per reference (m), part IV, paragraph 7.q.

(2) Contingency hours, for activated reserve squadrons using reimbursable funding, will be reconciled monthly between the active MAW, 4th MAW, and the MARFOR (G-3 for executed hours and Comptroller/G-8 for obligated costs). 4th MAW will identify by T/M/S and report the contingency hours and costs to the MARFOR that is providing the financial resources.

d. T&R flight hours lost (under executed or not executed) while supporting contingency operations shall not be flown in addition to programmed T&R hours for subsequent months of execution or flown in excess scheduled hours in other squadron(s) with same/similar aircraft or missions, unless mission requirements dictate.

e. Movement of under executed flight hours to satisfy T&R requirements for a squadron's lost hours should be done to create normal utilization of aircraft and to complete aircrew T&R requirements. Over-flying to meet total execution of Wing SBTP is prohibited. Each hour should reflect a T&R requirement and a corresponding contingency hours offsets.

f. Activated reserve squadron hours for contingency operations and CONUS training will be logged by aircrew, identified by T/M/S, and reported monthly to the TYCOM using their activated ORG code (listed in chapter 4, page 13 paragraph 14c) as coordinated by the MARFOR and MARFORRES/4th MAW. The MARFOR providing the financial resources for the activated reserve squadron(s) will report the executed hours and costs.

13. Frequently Used Financial Acronyms

AFM	Aviation Fleet Maintenance
AG	Activity Group
AIMD	Aviation Intermediate Maintenance Department
ALD-C	Aviation Logistic Division Aviation Supply
ASD	Aviation Supply Department
ASHE	Aviation Support Handling Equipment
AVDLR	Aviation Depot Level Repairable
BISOG	Blue (Navy $$) in Support of Green (USMC $$)
CLS	Contractor Logistics Support
CNAF	Commander, Naval Air Forces (see CNAP)
CNAL	Commander, Naval Air Forces, Atlantic
CNAP	Commander, Naval Air Forces, Pacific
CNRFC	Commander, Naval Reserve Forces Command
DFAS	Defense Financial and Accounting Services
FAS	Fleet Air Support
FastData	Fund Administration and Standardized Data Automation
FAT	Fleet Air Training (see FRS)
Fuel	Fuel funding Category
FHCR	Flight Hour Cost Report
FHP	Flying Hour Program
FHPS	Flying Hour Projection System
FRS	Fleet Replacement Squadron (see FAT)
GSE	Ground Support Equipment
IMA	Intermediate Maintenance Activity
IMRL	Individual Material Requirements List
JON	Job Order Number
MACP	Marine Aviation Campaign Plan
MALS	Marine Aviation Logistics Squadron
MARFOR (COM/PAC/RES)	Commander, U.S. Marine Corps Forces (Command/Pacific/Reserve
MF vans	Mobile Facilities vans
OAS	Other Aircraft Services
OMA	Operational Maintenance Activity Category
OMNR	Operational and Maintenance, Navy Reserves
OP-20	Flying Hour Program DON Budget Exhibit
PAA	Primary Aircraft Authorization
POM	Program Objective Memorandum (even year)
PPBE	Planning, Programming, Budgeting, Execution
PR	Program Review (odd year)
SAD	Aviation Supply Accounting Division
SAG	Sub Activity Group
TACAIR	Tactical Aircraft
TAD	Temporary Additional Duty
TBA	Table of Basic Allowance

TECOM	Training and Education Command
TL	Transmittal
TMS	Type Model Series of Aircraft
TOT	Transportation of Things
TYCOM	Type Commander

14. AC/RC Terminology Crossover

Active Component (AC)	Reserve Component (RC)
Budget OPTAR Report (BOR)	Flying Hour Cost Report (FHCR)
Fund Code 7B	Fuel
Fund Code 7F	Squadron Flight Equipment/Admin Supplies
Fund Code 7L	OMA and IMA Consumables Parts/Supplies
Fund Code 9S	AVDLR - Repairable Component/Assembly
Operational Functional Category (OFC)	Fuel, OMA, IMA and AVDLR
OFC-01	Fuel
OFC-09	IMRL/TBA
OFC-10	Other Aircraft Support, MF, EAF
OFC-21	TAD
OFC-23	TOT
OFC-50	OMA, IMA and AVDLR

Chapter 6

Contracts and Contract Maintenance Procedures

1. General. HQMC (DC AVN) is responsible for planning, executing, budgeting, and managing the Marine FHP for active and reserve components and serves as the service level advocate for FHP requirements within the Department of the Navy. The following paragraphs define procedures for the initiation, changes, and contingency requirement contracts for direct (AFM) and indirect (FO) funds. The purpose of this enclosure is to provide standardized procedures for the initiation of new contracts for funding considerations and updating contracts in place, prior and within the execution year. The core element of this Order is to standardize the reporting and monitoring of all contracts, direct and indirect.

2. MARFORs. Function as the resource sponsors with oversight authority and TYCOM-level representatives to validate and approve contracts involving manpower and contract maintenance for active component and activated reserve aircraft. MARFORRES will incorporate the requirements for reserve component squadrons based on guidance provided by CNRFC (N8).

3. Direct and Indirect Contracts. Contracts are defined by their impact to readiness and funding, direct or indirect.

    a. Direct Contracts. Direct contracts are documented as readiness requirements and directly impact the Cost per Hour (CPH) for specific T/M/S. Direct maintenance contracts must be validated via the Cost Adjustment and Visibility Tracking System (CAVTS) each fiscal year and submitted to HQMC (DCA) for approval and submission to OPNAV N4 for final approval inclusion into the annual budget process. No contracts will be approved without justification and approval by HQMC (DCA).

    b. Indirect Contracts. Indirect contracts are documented as readiness requirements but do not directly impact the CPH and are funded as level of effort with Flying Hour, Other (FO) funding. Indirect contracts will be reviewed at mid-year review for the upcoming year of execution. Expectations are that contracts will be reduced as new programs mature during normal transition of responsibilities to Marine Corps efforts. Programs deemed behind in training or delayed in implementation will be re-evaluated as required.

4. Emergent Contract Requests. New or emergent, and contingency operations requirements for Contractor Field Team (CFT) or contracts that are not captured as outlined in enclosure chapters (54) and (65), will be documented by the MARFORs and submitted to HQMC (DC AVNVN) via naval message with the following minimum standard information:

    a. Description of Requirement including applicable contingency operations or event(s) necessitating the requirement.

    b. Description of current manpower limitations or constraints (T/O, ASR, staffing goal, qualifications, etc.) necessitating CFT or augmentation support.

    c. Other mitigating options considered/applied and courses of actions.

    d. Specific number of contract personnel required with methodology for number of personnel required.

e. <u>Statement of Work</u>: Specific terminology of contract purpose and requirements.

f. <u>Longevity</u>: (Start/End Dates)

g. <u>Contract/Contractor Performance Metrics</u>:

(1) Aircraft Readiness level;

(2) Number of repairs or actions per month;

(3) Pass or Fail guidelines, if applicable,

(4) Acceptable levels of delays.

h. <u>Periodic Reviews</u>: Monitoring tools/reports.

i. Manpower/Force Analysis.

j. Reductions/Trade-offs (funding analysis).

k. <u>Total Cost with methodologyMethodology</u>. Man-hour cost/rate.

l. Exit Criteria.

5. <u>HQMC (DC AVN)</u>. Upon review and validation of the contracts, DC(AVN) will forward requirements to OPNAV, CFFC, and other commands as necessary for coordination and execution. MARFORs will incorporate the new CFT/contract into the existing quarterly and annual reports as required by enclosure 6.

6. <u>Contingency/Baseline Contract Overlap</u>. Contingency operations contracts costs, as outlined in chapter 4, paragraph 13., should not directly impact the direct Cost per Hour (CPH) for specific aircraft or FO accounts except in the current year of execution. Therefore, contingency support contracts (funded by FHP or FO) will not "overlap" or "piggyback" direct or indirect contracts funded by baseline OP-20 funds.

a. Contingency contracts will be generated for a set period of time with an expiration date not to exceed current execution end of year or 12 months, which will be reported quarterly and reviewed semi-annually, by the MARFOR (ALD) and HQMC (ASL).

b. Funding for contingency contracts will be exempt from end of year reporting for Cost per Hour (CPH) computation for designated aircraft.

c. Contingency contracts will not supplement or bridge contracts paid by baseline funding of the FHP.

d. Submission and approval process will be the same as new or emergent requirements.

7. <u>CAVTS Procedures</u>. Naval Air Systems Command/OPNAV Cost Adjustment, Visibility, and Tracking System (CAVTS) Procedures.

a. A Cost Adjustment Sheet (CAS) is created for each contract that is tied directly to an aircraft TMS and impacts the CPH. A CAS may be initiated at any level and forwarded through the appropriate chain of command to the cognizant MARFOR.

b.   MARFORs will submit the CAS via CAVTS website to OPNAV (N43), via HQMC (APP), for review and approval. Once approved, N43 will enter them into the budget. If not approved they will not be entered into the baseline CPH. All contracts will be reported to HQMC. Specific CAVTS information and worksheets may be obtained from the CAVTS website at http://logistics.navair.navy.mil/cavts/index.cfm.

Chapter 7

GLOSSARY

1. <u>General</u>. The following terms are vital to understanding the Flying Hour Program and the intrinsic tie between the T&R, funding levels, and unit level readiness.

2. <u>Definitions</u>

<u>Activate</u>. Order to active duty (other than for training) in the federal service. JP 1-02.

<u>Aircraft Program Data File (APDF)</u>. An 11-year projection that depicts the Primary Aircraft Inventory (PAI) for each unit funded under the aircraft-operating program. Provides the basis for budgeting documents used to provide funding for Naval Aviation operations, maintenance, spare parts, and manpower. It is a budgeting document, not a requirement document. PAI cannot exceed projected inventory in future years.

<u>Appropriation</u>. Authorization by an act of Congress that permits Federal agencies to incur obligations and make payments from the Treasury. An appropriation usually follows enactment of authorizing legislation. An appropriation act is the most common means of providing budget authority (see Budget Authority (BA)). Appropriations do not represent cash actually set aside in the Treasury; they represent limitations of amounts, which agencies may obligate during a specified time period.

<u>Aviation Depot Level Repairable (AVDLR)</u>. NAVICP Philadelphia manages 7R Cog repairable material that must return to depot for repair if they are beyond the intermediate maintenance level capability or declared beyond economic repair. AVDLRs are allowance items appropriated by NAVICP using NWCF funds approximately two years before the anticipated need of fleet activities to accommodate for long production lead times. Requisitioning of AVDLRs by squadrons using current FY O&M, N or, in some cases APN-6 funds for initial outfitting or changes in allowances, reimburses the NWCF and allows NAVICP to replenish material. Squadron expenses are reported on the monthly Operating Target Functional Category (OFC-50) Budget Optar Report (BOR) under fund code 9S. The OP-20 reflects AVLDRs under Special Interest Category (SIC) "FA" and is part of the Cost Per Hour calculations.

<u>Aviation Fleet Maintenance (AFM)</u>. Organizational and intermediate level maintenance funds granted to procure consumable parts, materials, tools, lubricants and services to repair aircraft, support equipment, or aeronautical components. Squadron expenses are reported on Budget Optar Report (BOR) under fund code 7L. The OP-20 reflects AFM under special interest category (SIC) "FM" and is part of the Cost Per Hour calculations.

<u>BISOG</u>. "Blue in Support of Green;" a term that identifies appropriations from the SECNAV level that support Marine Aviation.

<u>Budgeted Hour</u>. AN OP-20 term that defines how many hours or hours per crew per month (H/C/M) that are actually funded as a result of the PPBE process.

<u>Contract Maintenance</u>. Aircraft maintenance and support services outsourced to civilian or NWCF activities to support squadron operations when military personnel and/or equipment are not available or as economical as a Contract Field Teams (CFT). Contracts are written and approved at either the fleet

command level or NAVAIRSYSCOM and are financially managed at the TYCOM level. The costs are calculated based on fixed and variable estimates. Fixed cost obligate funds regardless of hours flown, while variable costs are determined by planned squadron hours. Contract Maintenance is seen as SIC "FW" on the OP-20 and is part of the cost per hour calculations.

Core Capability. A standardized measure of performance that a MAGTF Commander should expect during sustained contingency/combat operations. Combat flight operations define core capability in terms of daily-sustained sortie rate, or operational coverage, in support of a Mission Essential Task List (METL). This capability is the basis for the number of core skill proficient crews, and flight hours, required to maintain T-2 level readiness.

Core Competency Model. The basic structure which each T&R is built around. The Core Competency Model links community mission statements, METL, Core Capability Statements, Core Skill Proficiency and Combat Leadership requirements. The number of hours, or funding, required is determined by the number of aircrew necessary to execute the tasks stated in METLs and core capability statements.

Core Competency Resource Model (CCRM). Directly links the T&R program with the USMC flying hour and readiness-reporting (SORTS) program. It generates annual sortie and flight hour requirements (broken down by training, support, operational categories) for maintaining selected T-level readiness ratings for each tactical aviation squadron.

Core Model Minimum Requirement (CMMR). The minimum number of crews necessary in each particular core skill for a unit to accomplish its mission and METLs. CMMR and flight leadership requirements are the foundation of a unit's flying hour requirement and are a direct tie to unit level readiness.

Core Skill Proficiency (CSP). The number of individuals, or crews, required to be proficient in each designated core skill. An individual is considered Core Skill Proficient when they have completed, and maintain currency in, the requisite T&R syllabus for that particular core skill.

Cost Per Hour (CPH). The CPH represents the historical as well as the expected maintenance costs to train aircrews to fly one flight hour. It is a summation of fuel, AVDLR, AFM (consumables), and contract maintenance CPH. The historical CPH represents the actual cost reported by squadrons from Budget Optar Reports (BOR) while budgeted CPH signifies an OP-20 calculated estimate based on planned hours for each T/M/S. The budgeted CPH uses the last completed year of execution data as the baseline for OP-20 programming and then escalates the CPH by adjustment sheets, Center for Naval Analysis aircraft aging factor, NAVICP Logistic Engineering Change Proposals and NAVAIR contract estimates. (See definitions in this enclosure). Example: FY03 budgeted CPH was calculated using FY01 actual CPH and inflating it. FY04 budgeted CPH was calculated using FY02 actual CPH and inflating it.

Crew. As utilized for OP-20 and FHP purposes, a crew is the number of pilots required to fly an aircraft. For a single-piloted aircraft such as the AV-8B, a crew is one pilot. For a dual-piloted aircraft such as the CH-46 or KC-130, a crew is two pilots.

Flight Hour. A flight hour within the OP-20 represents the sum of Training, Support, and Operational hours. Calculating a flight hour requirement is dependent upon the schedule where the T/M/S flies its primary mission.

Future Year Defense Program (FYDP). A five-six year plan born from the PPBE process as a basic planning and programming tool that builds on a previously developed FYDP linking policy, strategy, and objectives to specific forces and major programs for all DOD components. The primary data element in the FYDP is the Program Element (PE).

Intermediate Level Maintenance. AFM functions assigned to ships, MAGs, and MCASs supporting aircraft and other designated aviation units that are separate from squadron (organizational) level routine maintenance functions.

Major Claimant. Budget Submitting Office (BSO) (e.g. CFFC) designated as an administering office under the Operation and Maintenance appropriation, which receive operating budgets directly from the CNO.

Mobilization. In accordance with Joint Publication 1-02 "1. The act of assembling and organizing national resources to support national objectives in time of war or other emergencies. 2. The process by which the Armed Forces or part of them are brought to a state of readiness for war or other national emergency."

Navy Working Capital Fund (NWCF). The NWCF is a revolving fund established to purchase stock material carried in the ship and MALS Supply Officer's stores. The MALS obligate NWCF dollars to provide items for stock issued to all end-use customers. The fund is reimbursed when material is issued for use by charging the customer's OPTAR and crediting the NWCF.

Operating Budget. The annual budget and financial authority of an activity or command containing the resources to perform its mission. TYCOMs subdivide their expense limitation(s) into various operating budgets. Some operating budgets are retained by the TYCOM (e.g., those operating budgets used to fund ships' TAD) and others are issued directly to lower levels of command (e.g., shore activities).

Operating Target (OPTAR). An estimate of the amount of money, which will be required by an operating ship, MAG, staff, squadron, or other unit, to perform the tasks and functions assigned. Commanding Officers may give subordinates a degree of financial responsibility paralleling their other responsibilities by the administrative procedure of issuing OPTARs for funds that are planned for utilization by the subordinate commander. OPTARs are administrative limitations and not legal subdivisions of funds, and the issuing commander retains all legal and accounting responsibility.

OPTAR Functional Category. A system whereby the various categories of O&M, N budgeting and funding are assigned a numerical designator. Each OFC supports a particular function/purpose.

Operations & Maintenance, Navy (O&M,N). An appropriation granted (or authorization) by Congress to Marine Corps and Navy operating forces to include the operations and maintenance of Marine Corps aircraft.

OP-20. A Department of the Navy (DON) planning document published by the Special Assistant for the FHP several times per year to establish the annual flying hours by T/M/S, which is used for FHP funding and fleet planning. Requirements are computed by using historical data and revised with MARFORs input. The OP-20 shows: required hours, crew seat ratios, force structure, and staff hours; budgeted hours; cost per hour by TMS; total costs by budget line item; and total T/M/S costs. See chapter 2 for detailed methodology.

OFC-01 Petroleum, Oils, Lubricants. Funding for POL consumed in flight operations, flight equipment, and squadron administration in support of the FHP.

Planning, Programming, Budgeting, and Execution (PPBE) System. A DOD decision-making process to allocate limited resources among many competing requirements within the services and between the services.

Program Objective Memorandum (POM). A biennial document that is a product of the programming phase of the PPBE. POM describes and recommends total DOD component resource and program objectives to SECDEF and is submitted only for even number years. Odd number years are called Program Reviews (PR). While POM cycles represent a new, complete assessment of all requirements across the FYDP, PR cycles are usually a revalidation of the POM.

Schedule A. An OP-20 category that identifies all Program Elements (PE) whose T/M/S primary mission is a TACAIR role. For the Marine Corps, this includes any MAG aircraft except FRS squadron aircraft.

Schedule B. An OP-20 category that identifies all Programs Elements (PE) whose T/M/S are within the Fleet Replacement Squadron (FRS) and whose primary mission is training of Category I-V pilots and aircrews.

Schedule C. An OP-20 category that identifies all Program Elements (PE) with T/M/S identified as Fleet Air Support (FAS) and whose primary mission is command and control and logistics support. Schedule C T/M/S are commonly assigned to the air station and are controlled by the COMCAB/MAW or higher command.

Schedule D. An OP-20 category that identifies all Program Elements (PE) with T/M/S assigned to MARFORRES/4th MAW.

Sortie. As defined in OPNAVIST 3710.7T, a sortie begins when the aircraft first moves forward on its takeoff run or takes off vertically from rest at any point of support and ends after airborne flight when the aircraft is on the surface and either.

NOTE 1:   The engines are stopped or the aircraft has been on the surface for 5 minutes, whichever comes first.

NOTE 2:   A change is made in the pilot in command.

NOTE 3:   For helicopters, a flight begins when the aircraft lifts from a rest point or commences ground taxi and ends after airborne flight when the rotors are disengaged or the aircraft has been stationary for 5 minutes with rotors engaged.

NOTE 4:   A sortie is primarily tied to a single aviation event, or T&R code; however it must be associated with a flight-time for purposes of planning and budgeting. The following flight times are the prescribed sortie lengths per T/M/S.

AV-8B	1.1
EA-6B	2.0
KC-130	2.0
AH-1W	1.5
UH-1N	1.5

CH-46E 1.5
CH-53E 1.5
CH-53D 1.5
F/A-18A 1.3
F/A-18C 1.3
F/A-18D 1.3

TYCOM. An intermediate level of command that is directly subordinate to the Combatant Commander. Financial authority is issued by major claimants to TYCOMs in the form of expense limitations.

Type/Model/Series (T/M/S). The specific designation of aircraft used by the military and used by the DON FHP for planning and funding. Type refers to the mission of the aircraft, such as attack (A), fighter (F), etc. Model refers to the particular airframe in that mission category, such as an F-18. The series is a particular configuration within the model, such as CH-53D. The series indicates equipment that is installed on board that gives it individual mission or performance capabilities.

APPENDIX A

MARFORCOM/MARFORPAC FLYING HOUR PROGRAM ADMINISTRATIVE CHAIN OF COMMAND
AND FLOW OF FUNDS

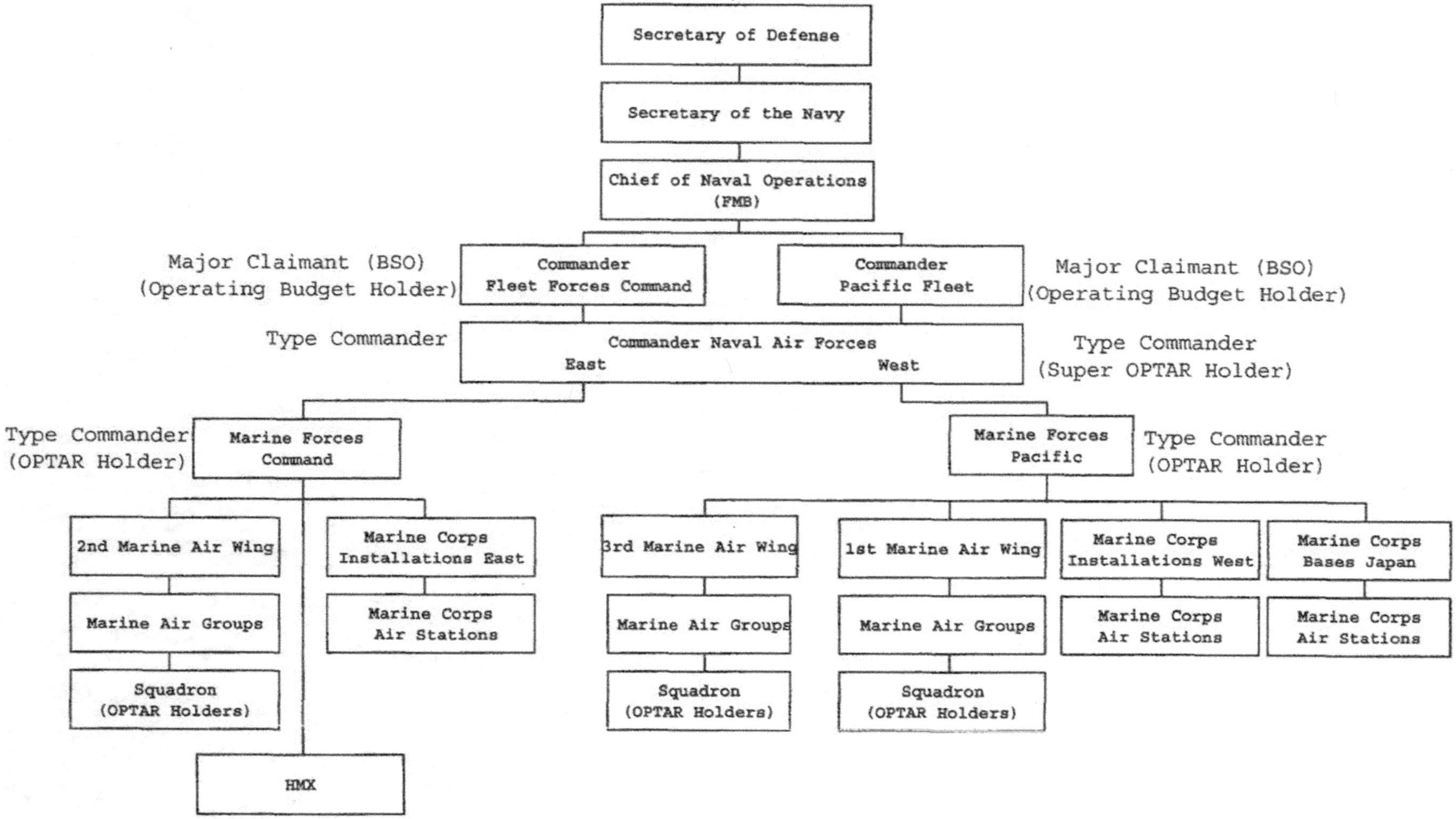

Secretary of Defense

Secretary of the Navy

Chief of Naval Operations (FMB)

Commander Fleet Forces Command — Major Claimant (BSO) (Operating Budget Holder)

Commander Pacific Fleet — Major Claimant (BSO) (Operating Budget Holder)

Commander Naval Air Forces East — Type Commander

Commander Naval Air Forces West — Type Commander (Super OPTAR Holder)

Marine Forces Pacific — Type Commander (OPTAR Holder)

Marine Forces Command — Type Commander (OPTAR Holder)

Marine Corps Bases Japan
Marine Corps Air Stations

Marine Corps Installations West
Marine Corps Air Stations

1st Marine Air Wing
Marine Air Groups
Squadron (OPTAR Holders)

3rd Marine Air Wing
Marine Air Groups
Squadron (OPTAR Holders)

Marine Corps Installations East
Marine Corps Air Stations

2nd Marine Air Wing
Marine Air Groups
Squadron (OPTAR Holders)

HMX

APPENDIX B

MARFORRES FLYING HOUR PROGRAM ADMINISTRATIVE CHAIN OF COMMAND
AND FLOW OF FUNDS

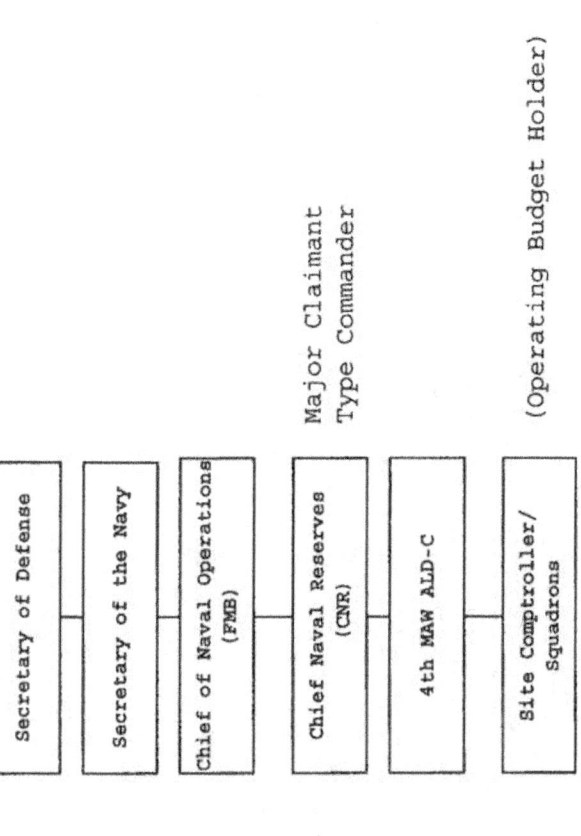